Teaching the Skills

JO PHENIX

Pembroke Publishers Limited

I dedicate this book
with love and thanks
to Neville Worsnop,
my husband, best friend, and greatest supporter.

© 1994 Pembroke Publishers
538 Hood Road
Markham, Ontario L3R 3K9

Canadian Cataloguing in Publication Data

Phenix, Jo
  Teaching the skills

Includes index.
ISBN 1-55138-034-X

1. Language arts (Elementary). 2. Language
experience approach in education. 3. Education,
Elementary – Aims and objectives. I. Title.

LB1576.P44 1994   372.6'044   C94-931830-2

Editor: Kate Revington

Typesetting: Jay Tee Graphics Ltd.

This book was produced with the generous assistance of the government of Ontario through the Ministry of Culture, Tourism and Recreation.

Printed and bound in Canada by Webcom
9 8 7 6 5 4 3 2 1

Contents

1

Introduction: Are We Afraid To Teach?

Sometimes we teachers seem to be like passengers on a sinking ship. First, we all run to one side; then, when the ship starts to tip dangerously, we all run back to the other side. Some of us like to jump on the latest bandwagon and think of ourselves as on the cutting edge of what is new; others view change as just another pendulum swing to quietly ride out.

Many of us began our teaching careers when teachers dominated their classrooms, when students were molded to match some norm or ideal, and when teaching to the course of study was paramount. Everyone was expected to do the same work in the same way and in the same time frame. We worked to "bring all the students up" to the level demanded. We, as teachers, and the textbooks we used were the sources of knowledge, and the students' job was to memorize information and give it back on demand.

New research into learning and child development made us question this kind of teaching. We realized that only certain kinds of information and certain kinds of learners suited a teacher-delivery system. We also realized that in many cases what we thought of as "learning" was superficial – it did not stand up in the real world. We discovered that learning was an active process in which the learner had to participate and take responsibility and that concepts were learned more by discovery, experience, and trial and error than by rote memory.

As a result, our classrooms changed. They became places where children engaged actively in doing things, rather than listening passively. The teacher became one who motivated and assisted learning, not one who prescribed and tested learning. We even called ourselves "facilitators." Instead of performing at the blackboard, the teacher became invisible, unable to be found in the classroom, always buried in a group of children. Teachers who stood up at the blackboard were considered reactionary, resistant to change, old-fashioned.

This was how the pendulum swung in the seventies and eighties. We took a great leap of logic, thinking that because direct teaching is not always appropriate, then we should not do it at all. In many instances, we went from a system where the teacher dominated to one in which the teacher stood back and simply waited for learning to happen. We believed that, because discovery and experience worked best for many kinds of learning, we should employ them for all kinds of learning. Once we recognized the importance of ownership, that learners should have control of and responsibility for their own learning, we believed that students should initiate all learning, that teachers had no right to make decisions about what a student should learn, or how the student should learn it.

We knew that our students had spent much of their time doing meaningless workbook exercises, performing repetitive tasks without a sense of real purpose, and we concluded that practice was inappropriate and that all assigned pencil-and-paper tasks were bad. We wanted our students to read literature by the best authors available, but when publishers bound together collections of this same literature into anthologies, we disparagingly called the anthologies "Readers," and often dismissed them as inappropriate.

Because we had learned that children develop at different rates, we concluded that they should never all write on the same topic, nor should they read the same story at the same time – we should individualize our programs. Some children worked on personal study labs or computer programs individually, checking their own progress as they went, and moving through a series of achievement levels. Yet few of these activities were child-centred. The content and methodology were predetermined, and the children had to come up with the same answers in the same sequence. But such activities gave the illusion of individualization.

We recognized that students have different needs and interests, so we made whole-class teaching taboo. We had learned about the value of group work, where students collaborate to discuss ideas, solve problems and accomplish tasks. We had learned that we must give individual attention to accommodate different learning styles and levels of ability. We drew the conclusion that lessons were now outmoded, that the teacher should never instruct the whole class.

This all-or-nothing approach to teaching has forced us to pick sides; it has made each side feel suspicious, if not hostile, towards the other. To rush from one extreme to the other shows only a superficial application of what we know about children and about learning. Often it leads to an abdication of our responsibilities in planning and guiding the learning experiences in our classrooms. If my English teacher hadn't forbidden me to use clichés, I would say something about babies and bathwater.

We now seem to fear that, if we open the door to skills teaching, we will automatically return to the sterility of rote-learning and workbook drill, that we will rush back to the other side of the ship. We should give ourselves more credit; we know more about children and more about learning than we did back then.

Perhaps going from one extreme to the other is part of our own learning process, a necessary step towards finding the middle ground where common sense can prevail. In my 30 years of teaching I have been many different teachers, from the didactic to the anarchic. In this book I intend to share some of my own experience, both of research and of children, and with the luxury of hindsight, try to make sense of it all.

> The biggest challenge we face in education today is to teach skills without losing the gains we have made in making our classrooms more child-centred.

2

Change: Why Can't We Go Back?

The Good Old Days

Did you ever talk to one of those people who had to walk 15 km to school, in the snow – and probably barefoot? Things were tougher in the old days, weren't they? These folk often think that because they lacked our modern conveniences they spent their time in school more profitably, showed more dedication to study, and somehow learned more of value. I'm inclined to think that under those circumstances I would have been half asleep all day. Many of us have selective memories about our schooldays.

I once appeared on a TV phone-in show in Thunder Bay, Ontario. A lady called in from a small, northern town to talk about the school train.* Apparently when she was a girl, the train, with the teacher, came around for five days every month. In between, the children did plenty of pencil-and-paper work and repetitive drills. Because this lady had grown up to be a keen and skilled reader, she thought the way she had been taught must be the right way. We all consider ourselves experts on school because we went to one.

In my local supermarket I overheard a couple of mothers talking about the upcoming school summer-vacation. One commented, "It must be really difficult for teachers because schools are so loosey-goosey these days." It seems people commonly believe that learning is less structured now, that kids do what

---

* School trains operated in northern Ontario until the late 1960s. A restored train is on public view in the town of Clinton, Ontario.

they like most of the time, that skills are not taught or studied anymore.

The idea that education was better "in our day" is not a new one. Writers in Greek and Roman times complained about declines in standards and the unruliness of the younger generation. *The Practical Speller*, published by Gage in 1881, says this: *"The pupils are turned loose on society to shock it by their bad spelling, and disgrace the schools which they attended, and in which they should have been taught."* It goes on to say that in a civil service exam in England at the time, poor spelling caused 1,861 out of 1,972 failures.

It's not surprising that classrooms mystify parents today. I was startled recently to realize that I am now in my sixth decade of personal experience with schools, from the forties to the nineties. Plenty has changed in that time. In fact, I have taken as my motto for life a sign I saw on the wall of a teacher centre in Transcona, Manitoba: There seem to be an increasing number of things I know nothing about.

The New Basics

The difficulty is that the skills themselves have changed. Schools used to teach mostly for the past: classics of literature by dead authors, history, dead languages. The ability to quote from these marked an educated person. Then we tried to bring things up-to-date, to teach skills that would be useful in the modern world and workplace.

The problem now is that we do not know what our children will need to know when they are ready to enter the labour force. Most people who now work with computers began school – or even left school – before the machines they use were invented. I left school without having mastered the telephone, and now I have to handle voice mail, call-forwarding and follow-me-roaming.* A person may now have two or three different careers during a working lifetime. We even often see retirement as the start of a new career.

We cannot view education as a list of things a person ought to know. Memorizing and parroting-back facts is no longer a

---

* I called my publisher this morning, and heard this recorded message: "You have reached our automated attendant." I could picture the robot at the switchboard.

useful skill – it probably never was. We can no longer even teach for today; we have to prepare our children for an ever-changing future. Fortunately, children adapt to change and novelty more easily than we do. In many households only they can remove child-proof caps or program the VCR.

So our classrooms today are different. We know that learning is something the children do for themselves, not something we do to them. Children no longer just listen to the teacher, they participate in their own learning. They don't just memorize facts and take tests; they create, solve problems, develop ways of working together, experiment. Quite often they make a mess of things, but don't we all when we are learning something new? I worry about students who used to get A all the time – how did learning something challenge them, make them struggle, bring them any failure? Anyone who succeeds all the time should do harder stuff, and that goes for adults as well as children.

It is no longer acceptable to train our children for the past – we must prepare them for the future. What our children need more than anything are the skills to find out for themselves what they need to know, the self-motivation to use those skills, and the ability to communicate and to solve problems. These are the basics we must go forward to.

Learning is, by definition, change, and it is a physical as well as a mental construct.

> We must beware of the "Back-to-the-basics" trap. Just what would we want to go back to?

3

The Child-centred Classroom:
What Other Kind Is There?

Curriculum-centred Education

When I began teaching, my classroom, in fact, the whole education system, was curriculum-centred. We had a course of study – we called it the syllabus – and we had to get through it. All the students studied the same topics, wrote the same essays, and took the same exams. And we judged all of them by the same criterion – how well they could write about the course topics. When we did our long-range plans, we divided the course up into weekly segments and made sure we never fell behind; if we did, we could not complete the course. If we taught efficiently, we wrote the end-of-term exam first, then made sure we covered everything that was in it; the students then had notes on everything and could memorize them for the exam. Students who missed school borrowed and copied someone else's notes. Students who could not keep up were left behind.

In this kind of system, the teacher decided ahead of time what the students ought to know and delivered the information, either personally, or by assigning readings. The students had to memorize as much as possible and give back the facts on demand. When I taught history under this system, I used the lesson time to tell the students about the topic. Then I assigned homework, asking the students to write down what I had told them. I then marked their papers to make sure they had told me what I told them, taking off marks for anything left out. Periodically, I tested them to see if they could remember what I had told them. If I tested without giving them fair warning, they would consider me unfair, because they had not had a chance to memorize the night before. I dominated the classroom.

We believed that the teacher meted out learning in manageable chunks and that scores on tests demonstrated learning. We evaluated our classrooms by the Pin Drop Test, believing that the students should be quiet and attentive and the teacher should talk. The emphasis was on correct teaching, and teachers were evaluated according to their performance at the front of the class. We've heard the story about the supervisor who came to evaluate a teacher, found her working with the children in small groups, and said, "I'll come back when you're teaching."

For some students this system worked. Those who could form concepts and make their own generalizations about the world by listening and reading could make meaning out of their schoolwork. Those who could understand written questions, had efficient short-term memories, and could write a coherent and organized first-draft under pressure did well on exams.

The survivors of this kind of education went on to university and became the leaders and decision-makers of the next generation. They naturally supposed that what had worked so well for them must be right for everyone.

But this system assumed all people learn in the same way and that students of any given age group can achieve at the same level if they work hard enough or spend time trying long enough. We know this is not the case. Children's cognitive abilities vary as much as their physical appearances; their methods of learning differ as much as their individual tastes and interests. Perhaps significantly, in my own curriculum-centred high school, we were all expected to dress alike and speak with the same dialect – uniformity in all things.

In a curriculum-centred system, students are graded according to how they match the norm: they are average, above average, or below average. The system is much like that of grading eggs or beef. We usually geared our instruction to the middle third of the class, the average. That meant two-thirds of the students were bored, either because we had not challenged them enough, or because we were teaching concepts too difficult for them to understand. Those who could not keep up had to stay after school to finish their work or take remedial help. Children soon learned where they fit in this scheme; often they adjusted their behavior in order to fit their mold even better. We had created a new disease: the Low-Group Syndrome.

We rejected this system because we learned more about how children learn. We discovered that learners participate in learning; they are not just told about it. We came to understand that meaning and problem-solving were at the heart of learning, not repetition and memorization. Most important of all, we realized that we were teaching children, not curriculum subjects.

What Does "Child-centred" Mean?

Child-centred learning is not a new methodology. It recognizes that learners are different and that the same content and strategies will not work for all. Our job is to find out as much as possible about each student's ways of learning so that we can give appropriate instruction. We must find out as much as possible about each child's interests and talents so we may use these to stimulate and enhance learning.

Child-centred learning recognizes that the **child** is our client, not the content of the curriculum, and not necessarily the needs of the community. It gives us the responsibility for ensuring that each child learns as much as he or she is able.

We should have worried more about our straight A students; they were not doing hard enough work.

Clearing Up Some Misconceptions

Misconception #1   Children determine their own rate of learning.

Children do learn at different rates. This fact of biology makes answering the question of expectations for different ages very difficult. It also makes it sometimes irrelevant. We can expect all we like, but the children can do only what they are capable of doing.

I have always found this concept of expectations well understood by the people who teach exercise classes. When I go to a health club, there are usually several grades of aerobic class, ranging from beginners-in-baggy-sweatshirts to experts-in-designer-tights. No matter which class I join, at first, I will be the only one who cannot keep up. I cannot do more than I am capable of – I will either hurt myself or quit in frustration. A good instructor learns what my limit is, then encourages me to push for just a little bit more each time. No matter how long a class exercises together, some people will always achieve more than others. If the instructor expected everyone to reach the same standard, failure would be built in from the start.

I need to feel that I am extending my own limits and making my own progress. In order to make this happen, most of us need a little help. We will not do that little bit extra unless we are guided and pushed. The reason we find exercising at home alone so difficult is that not bothering, finding excuses, or rushing through without working too hard is much easier.

Children learning at their own rate does not mean at the rate they choose; it means at the rate of which they are capable. We must assess what this rate is, and push each child to achieve the best possible results. The responsibility to do this adds greatly to the difficulty of teaching.

In the child-centred classroom, each child works equally long and hard and is equally helped and pushed. Each child, at times, and in equal measure, experiences success and failure, a sense of achievement and a sense of frustration. Overall, each child knows that he or she is acquiring new knowledge, learning new skills.

Misconception #2   Child-centred learning means no direct instruction.

For teaching to be child-centred, the methodology has to match the learning style of the child. Some of us can read instructions or owners' manuals and go off and do our assembly or repairs; others need a physical demonstration. Some people learn well from books; others learn better from other people, or through their own trial-and-error attempts. Some people can learn by listening, while others need to see pictorial representations or do hands-on work. There are many different methods of learning, and all can be successful. Most of us use a combination of many learning styles, while some of us lean heavily towards one particular style. A child-centred classroom matches the type of activity to the learning style of each student.

Methodology must also match the demands of the subject. If I want you to know the way to my house, I will not suggest trial and error. Group discussion may or may not lead to a helpful conclusion. A research project may yield results, but wastes a lot of time. I need to give you specific directions, and you should not show too much creativity in how you interpret them.

Depending on my personal preference, I may draw you a map or write out street names and directions. If you are a "map" person, one who works better from a diagram, you may have trouble following a series of written instructions; if I give a map or diagram to a person who prefers anecdotal information, I will not have considered that person's needs, and something is more likely to go wrong.

On the other hand, if I want to teach you how to make bread, I am not going to have you memorize the recipe or just watch me make the bread. I am also not going to try to describe how you know when you have kneaded the dough enough. If I am a good teacher, I will let you get your hands into the dough and feel the textures for yourself. Along the way, I will help you refine your technique, and give advice. I will also expect you to need a few sessions of practice to get it right, and that we may have to live through a few failures first.

I know this kind of learning has no shortcut. Learning by pencil and paper may train you to explain the methods, enable you to sound knowledgeable, or even score well on a written test, but it will not make you a bread-maker. I remember, as a child, asking my mother how I could know when the bread was baked, and she said, "When you can smell it." After 40 years of bread-making I have never found a better method.

Teaching is not a matter of picking a methodology and sticking with it. A child-centred teacher has a wide range of teaching methodologies and matches them, both to the individual students and to the subject in hand.

Misconception #3   Child-centred learning means no standards of achievement.

Standards seem to fit more with the evaluation we used to do, when students were compared with one another and with school or national norms, when our goal was to "bring all the students up" to the same level. In a child-centred classroom we know our students cannot all perform to the same levels. Does this mean we have no standards to work to? How will we know whether our students are doing well or not? Can we show parents where their children are, and how they are doing?

We need to know whether children are achieving or not before we can help them do better. The success of evaluation depends on what is done with the information. If we use the information just to label students, then it is negative and wasteful of everyone's time. If we use it in order to plan a more suitable kind of program, to use different strategies to help the student do better, then it is productive.

What we can do is to have our ultimate goal in mind. What is the end-product of education? What do we want our students to take away with them after their years in school? How do we define an educated person? Once we have our vision, we can back up along the years of school and picture what this educated person will be like at various stages along the way.

These staging points will give us the benchmarks of progress and learning. Our students may pass each of these staging points at different times in their school lives, but we have a similar goal for each of them. We want them to develop knowledge, skills and attitudes which will allow them to succeed both in their personal relationships and in their world of work and play.

There is nothing wrong with setting standards of achievement. Standards must be set and goals established, so teachers and learners know what they are striving for and whether they are making real progress. What is wrong is expecting that all children can meet the same standards at the same time. Believing in this impossibility builds in failure from the start. We must set goals and keep records of achievement for each individual. Then each learner has a good chance for success.

Misconception #4   Child-centred learning means the children make the decisions and choices.

Ownership is the key to successful learning. We only learn successfully those things we are interested in or really need to know. When we choose to study or learn a new subject or skill, we usually do better than when someone else imposes learning on us.

This reality does not mean that our students may choose whether they will learn or not. Nor does it mean that we have to wait until a student asks before we teach anything. It means that we need to make informed decisions about what is appropriate for students to learn. It also means we must create situations in which the students need the skills to be taught. When they have the need, then they will have ownership of the learning. A teacher does more than impart facts and knowledge – books, television and computers do that better – a teacher motivates and inspires others to pursue learning.

Decision-making is a shared responsibility. How to make informed decisions is one of the skills our students need to learn. However, the teacher must carefully structure choices and always control the direction of the learning.

Misconception #5   Child-centred learning is just for young children.

As we get older we become more able to learn abstract concepts, to generalize from experience, to learn vicariously through books and other media. We can often "think through" problems rather than having to act them out in play situations; we are able to understand ideas, situations and emotions through print without always needing concrete experience.

We still, though, have our preferred ways of learning. Some of us can solve math problems in our heads, others need to doodle on a piece of paper, others have to push objects around on the table. Some of us understand new information better in diagrams and lists than in sentences and paragraphs.

The rule for teaching is the same, no matter the age of the learner. We must discover to what extent our students can work in the abstract, and how much they need concrete experiences; whether they work best alone or in groups; what motivates them to learn. Whatever our age, teaching must match our learning style for us to learn successfully. No matter how old or experienced, we never become uniform.

> When I fly, I like to choose a passenger-centred airline. I don't want them to let me fly the plane.

4

Children: What Can They Teach Us?

Learning from the Children

I began my teaching life as a secondary-school history teacher with field hockey on the side. At that time, I found young children intimidating. When I came to Canada I began gradually working my way down through the ages, until I reached Grade 1. It turned out to be the biggest learning experience of my teaching life.

I had been told that young children have short attention spans. This didn't always seem to be the case. One child would spend all morning being an airplane, until I had to have him taxi up and down the hall a few times to give the rest of us some peace. Taking turns in the sand proved difficult, because they wanted to play there all day. They would spend hours trying to build a tower or act out a story. On the other hand, the activities I had laboriously spent all the summer creating for them were dismissed with a quick "I don't want to do that." I concluded that "short attention span" was a euphemism for *good boredom-detector.* Objects and activities have attention spans, not children.

My first mistake was to plan a classroom and a curriculum for children I had never met. I learned from my Grade 1 class that a classroom program must start with the students, not try to fit them in at the end of the planning process. Delayed gratification does not motivate children well. It's no good expecting them to learn things they may find useful at some future time in their lives. A task has to arouse immediate interest before they will focus much attention on it.

Children exercise the same discrimination I do as an adult. I don't have much of an attention span for things I find useless and boring. I give a TV program five minutes or so before deciding whether to watch it or not. If it hasn't engaged me by then, it goes off. I choose books in the same way. Life is too short to read a boring book. I read a lot of trash, but it is trash I choose.

When I went to teach Grade 1, writing particularly interested me, so I found myself spending a lot of time reading what the children wrote, and trying to figure out what it meant. What follows are two pieces of writing, both written by my students in October of Grade 1. They taught me some important things about writing, about children, and about myself.

A quick look at Kate's story tells us a number of things about Kate and her knowledge of language. I suspect she has been read to at home; she knows how stories go, and what they are for. She has a clear beginning, a series of anecdotes, and an ending with closure. Although she has written a personal narrative, we get the feeling that she has an audience in mind, with her humour and punchy ending. This writing leans into the realm of the poetic – it stands as literature.

Kate also knows a lot about print. Her printing is easy to read. She understands the concept of words and has spaces between the words. Her spelling shows an ability to sound out every syllable and to match it with a reasonable combination of letters, often very close to standard. She feels confident enough to try a word like *neighbourhood*.

Kate even knows how to put an apostrophe in, albeit in the wrong place. When I struggled to teach punctuation in Grade 7, I never imagined that they learned it as early as Grade 1. This apostrophe is a good sign. It shows that Kate has seen this in her reading, has made a generalization about language, and is trying to apply the rule in her own writing. Later on, she will learn when it is appropriate and when not. Frequent patterns are always learned first, exceptions later, and we just have to live with the miscues for a while.

This story was by no means typical of the writing in the class at that time. Most of the children were still drawing picture stories, trying out a few letter sounds or resisting doing any writing at all. I more often saw writing like this piece, by Paris.

Every day, Paris would bring me an incredibly messy piece of paper. His pencil had gone through the paper in several places. He would erase everything to a grey wash, then write over it. On the rare occasions when he used several sheets of paper, he would fasten them together with 100 staples; his writing folder already weighed 20 kg. When he brought up his paper, I would ask him, "What's your story today, Paris?" He would tell me in a few words, and that would be that. Paris did not shine as an artist, either. He never used crayons or markers, just a few squiggles with a thick pencil.

When a child hands in a piece of paper like this, we find it hard to know what it is, let alone what it means. But in the case of this story, I knew exactly what it was, because I watched Paris write it. I happened to notice him, all alone behind the piano. He was telling his story out loud and drawing on this piece of paper. The title was the first word I had ever seen him try to write: McDonald's. His storytelling sounded like a soundtrack, complete with dialogue and sound effects, and his scribblings on the paper were like punctuation marks in the story. When he had finished, he didn't even have a picture of his story. He had a page of randomly scattered objects, as if he had put everything in a bag and shaken it up.

The storytelling went on for about three-quarters of an hour, and during this time I managed to watch and eavesdrop without him knowing. When he finally brought me the paper, I said, as usual, "What's your story today, Paris?" He said, "Well, there was this robbery at McDonald's, and the cops caught the guys and put them in jail." That was all I got, for 45 minutes of complex storytelling.

Every day, in the classroom, I see work the children produce. Much of it is as different in appearance as these two stories. How should I respond? How should I evaluate? How can I help? What can I learn? How can what I observe make my teaching child-centred?

I learned something about the nature of writing. Comparing these two pieces, I can say very easily that Kate writes better than Paris. If by that I mean that Kate knows more about print and can present her story in a way that I can easily understand, then that would be true. Certainly, I have no complaint about Kate's story. It is wonderful. But what does writing well mean? If by writing I mean the ability to conceive and organize a narrative and generate language to express the ideas, then Paris is way ahead of Kate.

This discovery of Paris as a talented storyteller reinforced for me very strongly that writing involves two separate sets of skills. One set we call *composition*. This involves thinking up ideas or collecting information, then organizing the ideas, and formulating language to express them in a way that interests and informs a reader. The other set of skills we call *transcription*. This involves getting the composition down on paper in legible handwriting, using standard forms of spelling, and adopting a form which makes a good impression on the reader.

At that moment, Paris had virtually no transcription skills. Even his illustration could not convey his meaning. And when I asked him about his story, I could not reasonably expect him to go through the whole thing again. Paris turned out to be the most talented creator of stories I have seen in 30 years of teaching. By the time he had finished Grade 1, he had not only learned to print neatly and spell well, he had embarked on a series of Greek myths, including those about the twelve labours of Hercules and Paris, Prince of Troy. He spent long hours writing and rewriting the ancient stories which his mother told him, at home, in Greek.

I learned something about children. Paris' skill in composition was present in the story about the robbery at McDonald's – and in all those other scruffy pieces of paper I had dismissed as child-ish scribble. Because Paris had not yet learned enough letters to start creating spellings, I could not know about his talent just by looking at his writing. How many other times have I looked at a piece of work a student hands in and thought it represented the student's ability? How often have I evaluated solely by look-ing at product?

What Paris put on paper told me very little about his skill in writing. It told me about his lack of transcription skills and his need to learn some letter sounds so he could start preserving his language in print. It told me nothing about his creativity in com-position, his skill in organizing information, and his gift as a user of poetic language. That I discovered by accident.

I learned that if I wanted to find out what my students knew, I had to do more than look at final products. I had to be there while they were working, so that I could participate in the pro-cess, talk to them and listen. The writing conference offers this great benefit. As well as enabling us to help the students learn how to make their writing better, it allows us to listen in on their thought processes, to share their ideas, to give them another medium for showing us what they know.

Knowing whether a student can do a task or not is not enough. What really helps is to know how the student arrives at an idea, a piece of language or the solution to a problem. Students do very little at random. If they make errors, they usually have a logical reason. Students demonstrate what they know in many ways; I have to actively seek out those ways. Waiting to find out by acci-dent is not good enough.

What did I learn about myself? It is now several years since Kate and Paris wrote those pieces. I have shown the stories and talked about them many times in workshops. Each time I talk about them I seem to discover something new. Looking back, I know that at the time when I could really have helped these two children, I didn't know enough to do it.

Let's face it: studying two stories over a period of several years and then coming up with all kinds of deep insights into what they mean is easy. In the classroom, you may have only a few minutes, before you and the child are thinking about something else.

So what good is it? Well, for those two children, no good at all. I know now about the opportunities I missed to help the chil-dren, to say just the right thing, to teach just the right skill, to draw just the right conclusion. You see, I was doing what we all have to do. I was learning the craft of teaching as I went along. The first year I began teaching writing through individual conferences, I would end each writing session by wondering just what I had said that helped anyone. Usually I concluded, nothing. Like any other skill, teaching takes practice.

Making the Child Central

There are many things to learn to become a competent writer. There are many more to learn to become a competent teacher. We must resist a temptation to try to teach everything with every piece of writing the student does. When we try to eradicate all error and produce perfect pieces of writing all the time, we are falling into the trap of being writing-centred, rather than child-centred. A writing teacher must look at what the student is doing and decide what the student needs to focus on and learn about. In the early stages, the focus will likely be only one thing. Choosing the one thing that will help the student most at the time is part of the skill of child-centred teaching.

Teaching becomes child-centred when we learn from the children. To do this we have to look at work the child produces from the point of view of the child, not the task. The question I have to ask is not, "Has the task been completed successfully?" It is rather, "When I look at what the child has done, what can I deduce about what the child knows? What can I discover about what the child does not know yet?" In the light of the answers to these questions, I can make informed decisions about what I should teach.

In the case of Kate and Paris, for example, I can make a list of what each knows about writing. Each piece of writing they do will help enable me to build up a picture of the knowledge each has, and the skills each is able to use. If I have a good knowledge of the stages of development in composition, spelling, printing, punctuation, and all the other components of writing, then I can decide what each needs to learn next. Only in this way can I make sure I am teaching both what they need to know and are capable of learning.

I worry about all those years when I did not learn from what my students were showing and telling me; when I thought that seeing whether they did things right or wrong was what mattered;

when I didn't understand that I can't help anyone unless I know not just what they do wrong, but why they do it; when I thought I could evaluate knowledge and ability just by asking students to write something down.

Becoming skilled in interpreting children's writing requires that we read and talk about a lot of writing. Of course, we cannot go into great depth with every piece of writing a student does, or even with every writing conference. But I have always worked on the principle that doing something useful once a week is better than doing something useless every day. I believe we should make understanding writing a high priority. Not only does it have the potential to give us many insights about the students' thinking processes, it will influence greatly what we value, what we teach, and how we evaluate the students' progress.

> If we learn from our students, we can endow the act of learning with long attention-span potential.

5

Skills: What Are We Supposed To Be Teaching?

Different Approaches to Skills

The skills of any task are the things you need to know to succeed at the task. There are three main kinds of skills. Physical skills we can enhance through diet, training and exercise. Social skills we learn through interaction with other people and by analyzing and acting upon the response we get from them. Intellectual skills we foster through thinking and problem-solving.

Skills also tie in with specific tasks, such as carpentry or handwriting. These usually demand both physical and intellectual skills: we understand what the task is, practise the techniques involved, and apply them appropriately. We know that the interest in and ability to learn these skills is partly inherited and partly formed through experience. The nature versus nurture debate continues.

We can approach the teaching of skills from two opposing directions:

Direction #1

We can predetermine what the skills of a given task are, learn and practise them one at a time, and eventually put them into operation in a real situation.

When I was in high school we learned to swim by this method. Because we used the outdoor municipal pool, we had only the time from Easter to the summer holiday to be in the water. Miss Humm, the gym teacher, planned to save time by teaching us all the skills of swimming ahead of time. From

Christmas to Easter we learned to swim in the gym. We would put out the benches, lie across them on our stomachs and practise the breast stroke, first arms, then legs, then both together. We would hang by our hands from the wall bars and practise the leg actions of the backstroke. We practised breathing in unison as Miss Humm counted off the beat. We learned some theory about the dynamics of a body moving through water and about streamlining ourselves for maximum efficiency.

The problem with this method was that we did not really know why we were doing these strange movements. We were practising them in a medium quite unlike the water we would eventually enter. The fear-of-drowning factor didn't arise at all. I had never been to a pool, so had never seen swimmers up close. We had no way of knowing how successful we were unless we were told. And practice bored us; those of us who loved the usual gymnastics came to hate swimming practice. The odd thing was, even with all this preparation in the skills, when we got into the water we floundered around just as we had always done.

There was nothing wrong with any of the skills we were learning; all were important and helpful for a swimmer and we had to learn and practise them sooner or later. But separating skills from the real task they are designed to help tends to make drill a meaningless waste of time.

Much of our math teaching in the past has fallen into this same trap. We know that math in the real world consists of problem-solving. At home we estimate what we are spending as we go around the grocery store; we figure out how much wallpaper we are going to need; we check our gas mileage; we calculate our income tax. At work we engineer bridges, prepare budgets, make change, keep accounts. At play we total our golf score and do the mental arithmetic of card games. These kinds of tasks require that we have a good knowledge of the basic operations of arithmetic and of the fundamentals of algebra and geometry.

To plan our teaching and to write our textbooks, we made a list of all relevant skills, and introduced the easiest ones first. So, our young children first learned how to add, subtract, multiply and divide. Typically, we taught a skill, gave the children plenty of practice with sheets of exercises, and then assigned problems to be solved using the skill they had practised. Doing this sounded very logical and sensible to us at the time. The problem was, the children who were doing the pages of addition or subtraction had no idea why they were doing it. The hard part about math is not learning how to add, subtract, multiply and divide, it is knowing which one to do. This aspect received the least amount of practice. Children spent most of their time in school doing what a $7.95 calculator could do for them and little time on the real skill of math: problem-solving.

Of course, everyone needs to learn number operations. If we can remember multiplication tables and add up quickly and accurately we will save ourselves much time and trouble – and we won't always have a calculator at hand. But learning how to solve problems does not depend on accuracy in computation, any more than comprehension requires word-perfect oral reading. Accuracy in either computation or oral reading reflects a lot of experience and practice.

Computation is a tool of problem-solving. Problems are not created for the purpose of practising computation.

Direction #2

We can start with a task or problem and work towards learning and refining the skills involved.

To learn swimming by this method, we would first decide that swimming was something we wanted to learn about. Then we would get into the water, learn what it felt like, learn what effects it had on our normal body movements, and so on. We would watch what other people were doing and try to copy their movements. To become really proficient, we would find someone who knew more about it than we did and get some instruction. Each time we got into the pool, we would practise the skills we had been taught. Because we knew what we were trying to achieve, we would know how well we were succeeding, whether we were getting any better, and what we needed help with. Through modeling, instruction, self-evaluation and practice, we would gradually get better. If we worked hard, we might even become expert swimmers.

To help our students learn math this way, we might set up a store, start a business making cookies for recess, collect statistics on traffic flow in the neighbourhood, monitor the investment pages in the newspaper, or embark on any other project we thought would be within their capabilities and which might engage their interest and attention. As the project got under way, the students would discover what they needed to know and what new skills they needed to succeed. We would teach the skills as the need for them arose, and let the students practise them as they worked on their projects.

Whichever direction we choose, we are teaching exactly the same skills. We are also using many of the same activities and exercises. The difference is the meaning and purpose the students see in them. Meaning and purpose add up to motivation. To become skilled at anything usually requires much time spent in practice. The more motivated we are, the more time and effort we are likely to give to the learning, and the more successful we are likely to be.

What happened in my school swimming class was that despite all the work we had done in the gym, once we were in the pool we had to start again from direction #2. Isolating and preteaching the skills did not provide a shortcut.

Learning skills is rather like doing a jigsaw puzzle. Unless we can see the complete picture to know what we are aiming for, see the emerging picture unfolding before us, and have some idea of which pieces we are looking for next, we will find the task much more difficult, sometimes impossible, and always boring. If we start out with the problems and then search for solutions, the learning has an immediate purpose. Children can focus on meaning and problem-solving right from the start, and refine their skills as they go along.

I remember studying *The Merchant of Venice* in high school. As a culmination of the year we went to the London Old Vic to see a production of the play and the experience was wonderful. But all the way home on the bus, one thought kept running through my mind: we had just seen a play which lasted three hours, but had taken us eight months to read. All the analysis we had done, all the background information we had studied, and all the acting out we had tried would have made far more sense after we had seen the play. Plays are written primarily to be seen and heard, not read, but I suppose our teachers would have considered it cheating for us to know all about the play first. At least we got to see it before the exam, so we did finally find out how it ended.

Skills must be understood and learned in the context of their application in the real world.

> Meaning is what makes it possible to learn.
> It is also what makes it worthwhile.

Which Skills Should We Teach?

We have noticed over the years that skills lists never get any shorter. Every subject seems to have a growing list of skills. We have largely welcomed this growth because we have gone beyond the superficial skills we used to work with. Students must do more than perform mechanical repetitions in workbooks, or memorize words and facts out of context.

We used to have a very narrow definition of skills. Reading skills involved drilling phonics, memorizing words on flash cards, reading aloud without making errors, and answering comprehension questions about a reading passage. Writing involved learning grammar rules, analyzing sentences, naming parts of speech, and fixing up spelling and punctuation mistakes.

Now that our skills are more complex, making sure that we are covering them all is more difficult. Simply listing all the skills we want our students to learn is not useful. Doing so would give us too unwieldy, too intimidating a list.

I find it helpful to think of skills in three main categories:

- Skills of Meaning: Engaging in the task
- Skills of Process: How to go about the task
- Skills of Content: What you need to know

Skills of Meaning

For real learning to take place, the learner must make a commitment to learn. True and lasting learning cannot be imposed from outside. Going through the motions of completing a task does not guarantee that learning is taking place; it can often work against learning, especially when the learner lacks interest in the outcome.

How many of us, after our own experiences with literature in high school, vowed to read trash for the rest of our lives? How many gave up reading altogether? We didn't call it "doing" poetry for nothing. We spent so much time analyzing the techniques and writing exam questions on who wrote what and why that we gained little appreciation for the beauty of poetry, or of its potential significance in our lives. Nor did we appreciate or learn the skills that writing and reading poetry require.

Of course, our appreciation and enjoyment of any subject increases as our knowledge about the subject increases. Appreciating the first baseball game or cricket match we ever see is hard. Although the excitement, the smells, the spectators may draw us in, we don't really know what is happening. However, once we know what the players are doing, understand the tactics of the game, and start to translate the language into recognizable English, then we can enter into the fun. We may even become fans, which will ensure that our knowledge and understanding will continue to grow and develop. Can you imagine your first experiences of baseball consisting of the analysis of short segments of a game on videotape, or a list of the rules of play to memorize? That would hardly motivate you to buy a season ticket.

Similarly, we can enjoy literature more if we know about the techniques and look more closely at the words and the language. But we must get to the meaning first. We must appreciate literature on a personal and sensory level before moving on to analysis. Our knowledge and appreciation then grow as we read more, experience more.

If we want students to buy season tickets to learning, then we must engage them first in the tasks at hand.

This does not mean we have to wait for the students to come up with something they want to learn about. We never waited until long division came up in a child's daily life! Our main job as teachers is to widen students' horizons and introduce them to ideas, concepts and skills they would not think about otherwise. We are responsible for making informed decisions about what our students ought to learn. After all, we know more about the world outside than they do, and we want them to be ready for it.

Of course, we will capitalize on the students' interests in order to teach them skills. They will learn more about reading if a book interests, rather than bores, them. They will acquire more research skills if they really want to find out about the topic. They will take more trouble with spelling and neatness if they care about the impression their writing is going to make on an audience. I have never seen children learn to add and subtract in their heads so quickly as when I taught my two nieces how to play blackjack.

Motivating students, a prerequisite for all learning, is the most important part of teaching. Anyone can deliver information, give out assignments and mark correct answers and a computer can do it better. Sparking a child's desire to learn needs a personal touch.

The science of teaching is knowing what the skills are. **The art of teaching** is making the students believe they really want to learn them.

Skills of Process

The process or product question has also had us picking sides.

In the old days, product was all that mattered. We checked the math and counted the right and wrong answers; we checked the spelling and marked it right or wrong; we treated all writing as final draft, and evaluated it for correctness and neatness. We measured performance by scores and marks. For summative evaluation, we averaged out the marks for every piece of work a student had done. We began with a view of what a good product was and deducted marks for anything that fell short of this. We worked with a deficit model.

Process means how we go about the task at hand. It is all about how to achieve the product we want and about having a variety of procedures to enable us to do that. For example, we can solve a math problem in different ways. We might move objects round our desktop, draw a diagram, make pencil-and-paper calculations, or use trial and error.

A process approach recognizes that writing does not come out perfect the first time, that revising and editing are a natural part of writing. We need to know that if we meet a word we cannot read, we can take a guess, or skip it and read on.

Process also involves planning and organizing our time, information and materials so we can work efficiently and complete the tasks we have set ourselves.

No one can achieve a product without understanding the processes involved; process and product cannot be separated.

Misunderstandings about process arose among teachers and among parents.* When we believe in the importance of process, we often get a product that is less than perfect. Spelling may not be corrected; a final draft may not be done; credit may be given for getting a math problem only partly right. Sometimes, such responses are taken to mean that we are lowering our standards, that we are settling for less than the best, that our students are learning sloppy work habits.

The misunderstandings revolve around the issue of focus. Good teachers know that students are more likely to succeed in learning if they can concentrate on one thing at a time. Writers know the importance of focus too. That is why the drafting process works so well – it lets us attend to one aspect of writing at a time, instead of trying to think about ideas, language, style, spelling and handwriting all at once.

When I work with a student on a piece of writing, we both strive to make that writing the best it can be – to finish up with a good product. In order to produce a piece of writing, a writer must focus on the product at all writing stages. With a goal in mind, the writer makes decisions about what to include, what kinds of language are appropriate for the audience, what the best way to organize the facts is, what need for pictures or diagrams exists, what form the final draft will take. As a teacher of writing, I help my students to focus on the product, in order to help them shape and improve their writing. The level I work towards will depend on the age and experience of the student.

As a teacher, though, my real focus differs from the student's. I am not teaching for today, but for the future. Looking only at product is short-sighted. In the large scheme of the student's life, any one piece of writing will probably be unimportant, perhaps forgotten by next week, or even by recess. I do not usually care about the particular story or report I am reading. In my long-term plan, I care about what the student is learning about writing. The learning that lasts is not the content, organization or language of this piece of writing, however good the product. It is the understanding of how writers write, of how they think and work.

My goal is that the student will learn skills and ways of

---

* And perhaps also among students. Did they also learn that finishing up with a good product was unimportant?

Xmas
1947
This brings
my love
and best
wishes
to Mummy
and Daddy— a very happy
Christmas to
you both.
With lots of love
from
Josephine

This is one of the first pieces of "writing" I took home from school. It was the kind of product valued then. Nothing personal appears on the page; every child copied the same words the teacher had composed and printed on the board and decorated the page with cutouts from old Christmas cards. The teacher took no chances with young children's own language and illustrations. We learned nothing about writing.

working to apply in the future. A bulletin board full of perfect scores or neatly drafted stories might look nice today, but what good will it do the students in the real world of tomorrow?

Through the individual pieces of writing my students work on, I teach the processes of writing.

Similarly, with early readers, providing reading materials with controlled vocabularies and training children to read aloud with word-perfect accuracy is easy. Such oral reading always impresses listeners. However, the real skills of reading have little to do with correctly reading words out loud.* Most reading in the adult world is done silently, and saying or even looking at all the words is unnecessary and often hindering.

Sounding good today is only a short-term goal in reading instruction. As a teacher of reading, I need to focus on what the child is learning about the nature of reading. The goal of my reading lesson, then, is not that the child gives a good performance today, but that the child learns strategies and procedures that can be used when he or she is alone with a story. The child needs to think and act like a reader, in other words, to understand the process. Each reading experience I design for the classroom will teach the students about the processes of reading.

The process **is** my product.

Skills of Content

Content is information. Information is the raw material we use to complete tasks and to solve problems. For each subject we teach we have in mind a list of things we think students ought to know. This content grows continually. Not only does our civilization keep learning more and inventing more, society is constantly identifying new subjects and problems for schools to deal with.

As students grow older, content tends to play a larger part in the curriculum. Students reach an age when they can move away from immediate personal experience, and learn vicariously about the larger world around them.

---

* Fluent oral reading is a specialized skill. We use it when we read aloud for our children. TV and radio newscasters are professional oral readers. In these instances, oral reading is a performance, much like that of an actor. It is often carefully rehearsed.

Content used to be established by a course of study devised by our school or board, by external examinations, or by the particular textbook we chose to use. As our dependence on textbooks decreased, we became more and more responsible for determining for ourselves what content we ought to teach.

When computers first became available in schools, the board of education I worked for set up a series of workshops so teachers could learn computer skills. In the workshops they taught us all about how computers work and how we could program them. We did little programming exercises; all I can remember is typing "goto" a lot. A couple of people found this really interesting. For most of us, though, we did not want to know how computers work, but how we could make them work for us and for our students.

I have used a computer in my work now for more than 10 years. I do not know how it works any more than I know how my car or my electric lights work. I don't care. I do not want to write my own programs or build my own car. I have learned the skills I need to use for my daily work, and I have found this onerous and time-consuming enough.

The computer courses we took years ago did more to scare us away than to make us computer literate. There was nothing wrong with the skills or the instruction, but for most of us, it was the wrong information at the wrong time.

Understanding the subjects we teach, and knowing what might help the learner, can help us make decisions about the when, how, and how much of skills teaching. This knowledge can help us avoid controversies like those we have suffered over such thorny topics as phonics and grammar.

The Great Phonics Debate

To decide on the skills students need to learn in any given subject, we need to have a good understanding of the subjects we are teaching. Take, for example, the **Great Phonics Debate**.

We have learned that there are three main groups of skills we use as readers. We call them cueing systems. One focuses on context and our prior knowledge of the subject we are reading about. One focuses on patterns of language and our knowledge of grammar, word order, etc. The third focuses on print symbols and their link to the sounds we hear in words. We use all three of these groups of skills in varying degrees every time we read. If we are weaker in any one of the three, our reading will be unsuccessful.

We got into a dilemma because for a while we subscribed to a view of reading in which learning to sound out or recognize all the words was seen as a first step to reading success. *McGuffey's Eclectic Readers*, first published in 1879 and widely used in North America, advocated a combination of the Phonics Method and the Word Method to teach beginning readers. Reading series introduced in the mid-twentieth century, featuring duos like Dick and Jane, Janet and John, and Tom and Betty, sought to teach children to memorize all the words before meeting them in print.

These methods reflected the belief that the only ways to figure out a printed word were to sound it out using phonic rules, or to memorize it beforehand. Teachers evaluated reading proficiency by listening to a child read aloud and counting all the errors. They measured reading achievement by considering which book the child was reading at any given time. They saw saying all the words right as the first and most important reading skill. Beginning reading skills were called *word attack skills* – it was as if students had to wrestle reading into submission.

These reading series were designed on a kind of scientific model, everything preplanned, every word-choice justified. At first glance there seemed to be a certain logic about them. Certainly, good readers can usually sound out unfamiliar words and recognize many words in isolation. Unfortunately, cause and effect got confused. Word accuracy comes as the result of a lot of reading; it is not a prerequisite for it. Being able to recognize and say words does not necessarily make you a reader.

As a result of our new understanding of the reading process, we changed to a different approach. We used stories with real and meaningful language, rather than controlled vocabulary. Aware of the different kinds of cues a reader can use to figure out words and meanings, we focused our teaching on the meaning rather than on word accuracy.

We assumed that teaching phonics was no longer necessary, that children would pick up a knowledge of print as they went along. We even considered teaching phonics counterproductive. Whenever my young students misread my name and called me "Miss Phonics," I felt embarrassed.

Many children learned to read successfully without phonics instruction. They made the necessary generalizations about how print works and moved quickly into reading. Other children seemed unable to get started, and many others did not progress beyond the beginning stages.

We had once again made an "all-or-nothing" decision. But recognizing that meaning comes first and is of prime importance does not mean we should avoid teaching skills of phonics and word recognition. Of course we should teach them. It's not an either/or situation. Some children and some adults do not readily notice patterns or recognize the logical ways our language and words are constructed. (This is why many adults cannot spell, despite many years of reading and writing.) These children would find it helpful to have their attention drawn to letter patterns and word structures.

Many people fear what would happen if we admit phonics teaching is a good idea. They wonder if teachers would get out the old phonics workbooks again and go back to dealing with letters and sounds out of context. Surely we know better than that now. We know that we must ensure that the children see the connection between these skills and real language, real literature, and real experiences. Real reading and writing provide meaning and purpose for learning the skills, and we know that learning things that are meaningful is easier than learning things that are not.

The question is not whether we should teach phonics or not, but when and how and to whom we should teach it.

Those of us who have watched young children struggling with the print system know that it is in writing that they really need a good knowledge of how letters and words work. Writing demands that you construct words, not just recognize them when you see them. Before children can try any spellings, they must have some basic knowledge about letter sounds – a beginning writer can make a few consonant sounds go a long way. By using their letter and sound knowledge as they try to spell, children learn the intricacies of the phonic system. When children read, however, they use context cues, pictures in the text, and their knowledge of language structures as well as phonics to understand what they are reading. Beginning writers have only their knowledge of phonics to help them construct words.

For my six-year-old students, writing time was concentrated

phonics practice. I could hear them saying and listening to every sound of every word they were trying to write. After this, they found recognizing the letters and sounds in reading easy.

So if we want children to understand how sounds and symbols work in print, we will teach phonics mainly as a spelling skill, not as a reading skill.* Phonics will be learned and practised where it is really needed – in word-construction.

We should not talk about a phonics approach, or a whole-language approach, or any other kind of approach. *Approach* suggests an abnormal emphasis on one set of skills over another. We need to understand how and when readers and writers use the various skills and to develop a program that encompasses them all. To keep rushing backwards and forwards from phonics to whole language takes us back to the sinking ship analogy. The children are likely to sink in the middle.

---

* We must always give children consistent messages about print, whether they are encoding or decoding. Many parents who favour a phonics approach to reading and who look for word-perfect accuracy in their children's reading are horrified when their children use this same phonic information to create spellings that are not standard. If phonics is important in understanding print, then it is important in all print. After all, we read writing, and write reading; writing and reading are not two separate uses of print.

Tun we Pad basble
weT My FRvc
saN we Pad Feble
weT MY PRive
saN we ~~Pad~~ Otda-Ras
weT MY FRNe

Then we played baseball with my friend.
Then we played football with my friend.
Then we had a race with my friend.

Colleen is using her knowledge of phonics to construct words as she writes. Because she hasn't had time to learn many sound patterns yet, she uses a combination of letter sounds and letter names to write her story.

- She has represented most consonant sounds correctly: n, p, b, l, w, m, f, d. Children usually learn consonant sounds first, because they are easier to distinguish from one another and fairly consistent in the sounds they represent.
- She uses letter names to represent long vowel sounds, like the *a* in *basble* and *ras* and the *e* in *we*.
- She has not yet learned about short vowels. When she wants the short *i* sound in *with*, she goes back to saying the alphabet, and chooses *e*, the closest sound she can find.
- For the short *e* sound in *then*, she chooses *a* again, the closest she can get by saying the names of the letters.
- She hasn't yet learned that sometimes two letters represent one sound, like the *th* in *then*. She chooses *z*, the closest sound she can hear.
- She knows the spelling of *my*, probably as a sight word.

The more Colleen learns about phonics, the better she will be able to construct words according to sound patterns.

Grammar Questions

If phonics served as the foundation of reading, grammar once played the same role in writing. Writing instruction used to centre on grammar. We taught subjects and predicates, parts of speech, punctuation and verb tenses. In fact, we spent so much time on these sub-skills, students had little time to write anything. Creative writing was at 2 p.m. on Thursdays, if nothing else got in the way.

Much was written about the teaching of writing in the seventies and eighties. We took the new insights to heart, introduced personal writing into our classrooms, and made sure students had a good block of writing time every day. Students wrote as they had never done before. Freedom from standard spelling allowed even our youngest children to write, using all the richness of their own speaking vocabularies. The old, analytical grammar died a natural death. Some curriculum documents even forbade the teaching of grammar until the teenage years. We put our faith in the quantity of writing students were doing, thinking that through it they would learn all they needed to know about using written language.

My first experience in breaking away from the old skill-drill-kill method of teaching grammar was with 11- and 12-year-olds. These students were neither high achievers, nor keen writers. In their assignments their writing was dull, routine, and repetitive, and as short as they thought they could get away with.

My school initiated a program in which students had to do personal writing every day. This meant that for the first time in their lives those students had to write daily, without specific assignments or topics to choose from.

At first, they went into withdrawal; many wrote nothing at all in their writing time. But after they got tired of sitting doing nothing, they began producing writing that was magical. They wrote poetry I could not have dreamed of asking for and personal stories that would make me weep.

Both the quantity and quality of this writing astounded me. We teachers felt very good about what we were doing.

Actually, we weren't doing much. All we did, and it was a big step in letting go of control, was to give students the freedom to do what they were capable of. We did not restrict them to textbook tasks. Looking back, I can see the big hole we left. We created a climate that generated a great outpouring of writing and then we did nothing with the writing. We accepted that marking all the errors and putting a score on the writing was likely to make students reluctant to write. We encouraged risk-taking, and took care not to criticize students' efforts. However, we also abdicated our responsibility to help the students do better.

We thought that doing the writing was enough. How many chances did we miss, when we could have stepped in and said, "I see what you are trying to achieve here, and I can show you a way to do it better"?

Many parents did not understand our new philosophy. When they talked to their children, they discovered the children did not even recognize words like *adjective*. Parents made comments like, "How can they write when they don't know what a verb is?" We tried to explain that knowing the names of parts of speech and clauses was unnecessary in order to write, that all children who could talk understood the basics of grammar.

We tried to take an individualized approach to teaching writing. We introduced writing conferences to allow us to work with students individually while their writing was in progress. We discovered that talking about a piece of writing in progress was the best way, sometimes the only way, to help students improve as writers. But without any common terminology, we could not talk about certain aspects. We were not allowed to teach students about parts of speech. *Noun* and *verb* had become four-letter words.

Our fear of these words was understandable. We used to teach them by having students underline words in sentences, and by doing workbook drills. We tried to teach the terminology before students understood the concepts. We did not give students enough experience with the concepts before plunging them into exercises they could not do. Most of our teaching was divorced from any real writing the students were doing. It seemed we could only get out of our bad habits of the past by eliminating grammar completely.

We now fear that if we give approval to teaching grammar again, some of us will get out the old grammar books and go back to the futile and wasteful teaching of the past.

But to talk to students about their writing, we need words with which to do it. By introducing grammar terminology, we can enable students to understand parts of speech and the syntax of our language, something that, as writers, they will find very helpful.

Grammar does not have to be boring. Words can fascinate us, and the more we know about them, the more interesting they become; we must have worked very hard in the past to make them boring for our students.

We know enough now to keep the teaching of grammar in touch with the students' own reading and writing; we can also teach through experience with language, rather than through isolated drills. And we can focus on putting our own language together, rather than taking someone else's apart.

What made us think that saying *describing word* was easier than saying *adjective*? Students still have to understand the concept. If they understand a concept, they can learn the name for it. If they can learn names for such abstract concepts as joy and intelligence, they can learn the much simpler concepts they use every time they speak.

Very young children learn the concepts and names of *word* and *sentence*, which are far more abstract and difficult to learn than *noun* and *verb*. Children learn the concept of *word* quite easily because they hear the word used in context every time they talk about reading or writing. They can learn *verb* just as easily, if they hear the word used in context many times.

We must not fear teaching children the content skills of language. We are good enough now to use effective methodology and to make the words meaningful and useful for our students.

> Students need not reinvent the wheel every day.
> Skills of content can be taught and practised.

6

Learning: What Helps?

Making It Easy

David Frost once said that the American dream is to grow up, get married, and make a home for major appliances. I think this is why I have adapted very well to North American living. Where is the virtue in doing things the hard way?

Perhaps civilization is all about making life easier, finding better ways to do things. But I remember my teachers fighting a rear-guard action against this trend. When I began school, we wrote on slates. (I'm not *that* old – schools were poor in post-war England.) Pencils and paper we used only for practising penmanship. We never got to compose anything, but if you saw any of the samples my mother saved from my first year, my printing would impress you. The second year, we were allowed to use paper regularly. Along with the paper, came the dip pens.

We had to master several skills in order to use the dip pens. First, we each had to make a pen-wiper, a ritual on the first school day of September.* Then the pens were given out. We sat at the kind of desk you see in pioneer villages – double occupancy, lid that sloped down towards your lap so everything slid off, and a porcelain inkwell in the top right-hand corner. (Desk designers saw no need to help left-handers.) We had to dip our pens in the inkwell, carry them over to the paper without dripping, and start

---

* To make a pen-wiper, you cut half a dozen layers of felt into 10 cm (or 4 in.) squares. Then you stack them up and stitch through the centre a few times. After writing, you insert your pen between the layers, and wipe it clean.

writing. No matter at what angle we held the pens, they sputtered and threw blots all over the page. When we started to write, we had nibs full of ink, so the first couple of letters came out heavy and blotchy, the remainder gradually fading away to nothing. Consequently, our writing finished up as a series of print chunks, the pattern going from dark to faint, then jumping to dark again.

Out in the real world, most people had adopted the fountain pen. Even though this pen did a better job and made less mess, we were not allowed to use it. I think the teachers thought it made writing too easy. When I got to high school, we were allowed to use fountain pens, having done the righteous thing and learned to write the hard way first. At about this time, though, the general public had switched to the ballpoint pen. We were not allowed to use it in school. Somehow the ballpoint pen was for lesser mortals that we grammar-school girls.

A later generation of students had the same problem with the pocket calculator. Somehow adults deemed it okay for their use, but not for children's. The idea seemed to be that unless students did their arithmetic the hard way, they would not learn as much. But calculators don't do the hard part. Knowing how to add or subtract or multiply or divide is not the hard part. Knowing which one you are supposed to do is. Give students a page of addition or division problems, and they are all right. It's when you mix the operations up that the trouble starts. No calculator will help them then. If they don't have a good understanding of mathematical concepts and a few problem-solving strategies, the calculator cannot help them. What the calculator can do is allow them to focus on the concepts, without having to worry about the computation at the same time.

Only give a student one hard thing to do at a time. After all, in math, computation is only a means to an end, not the end itself. Whether students get the right answers today matters less than whether or not they will be able to solve problems tomorrow.

We have sometimes, though, allowed computation to become an end in itself; we have allowed our students to believe that mathematics revolves around such things as knowing tables and number facts. Doing this makes as much sense as defining writing in terms of knowing which way *b* faces. It's important information, but not central to the task.

I believe the thinking behind this attitude is summed up by

a comment I heard a board of education superintendent make about the use of computers in schools. The superintendent said that computers should not be used before Grade 4, because children should learn to do things the hard way first. In her novel, *Devil on My Back*, Monica Hughes describes a learning system in which people interface directly with computers through surgical implants. Doing this allows access to a vast amount of knowledge without the necessity of years of study. Education in this future society focuses on ways to link and use information. What if we could really do this? We are scratching the surface of these techniques with sleep-learning and hypnosis. Would we welcome the new and improved ways of learning, or would we think the learning less worthy because students could acquire it too easily? The fight over the ballpoint pen could be a minor skirmish compared to any battle provoked by this issue.

Whatever kind of learning theory says that we should do hard things first? It seems to me that if we want to enable our children to learn successfully, then we must make learning as easy as possible.

There is one way in which we have always tried to make learning easy. We break tasks down into manageable chunks and put them into a logical sequence. The theory is that in this way we can build up knowledge gradually, each new piece fitting into existing frameworks. This makes good sense. But how do you decide what students should learn first and how the sequence should continue?

Have you noticed that when you play Trivial Pursuit, the other people always get the easy questions? Why is this? What makes a question or a problem easy or hard? The only rule, as far as I can see, is that if you know the answer the question is easy, and if you don't, it is hard. Figuring out what someone else will find hard or easy is tricky. Perhaps we can learn from our own experience.

The things we learn most successfully are, first of all, things we ourselves choose to learn. These things we either need to know about to get along in the world or are interested in. When we want to learn, we do not necessarily find the task easy, but we are prepared to spend time and energy in order to succeed. Learning becomes harder when it is imposed on us, when we are not particularly interested in the subject, and when we have no immediate need for the skill or knowledge. In this case, we spend the minimum of time and effort, experience more frustration, and succeed less often.

The art of teaching is to create in the students a *need* for the skills we want them to learn, then engage them in interesting ways to acquire and practise those skills. For the learner, need and interest must come first, in order to make learning as easy as possible.

In the Dick and Jane system of instruction, children learned words by rote, while in phonics-based programs they practised sounding out. Neither the sounding out nor the memorization were linked to real reading experiences. Reading material for early readers presented words in an orderly sequence, and a reading lesson offered phonic and/or memorization practice. The idea was that when students had memorized enough, they could move on to real reading, a problem-solving activity. And teachers could evaluate students' reading progress by considering their ability to recognize and say words correctly.

The problem was that without real reading to start with, decoding skills were unnecessary. Reading became another rote-memory operation without real purpose or incentive. Of course, knowing about sound-symbol relationships will help a reader, but it is only one tool among many to get meaning. Means and ends were confused.

We fell into the same trap in writing instruction. We concentrated on neat handwriting, accurate spelling, and memorized grammar rules as the raw material for successful writers.

Now we recognize that these are only tools of the composing process. Like math and reading, writing is a generative, problem-solving activity. Until students focus on composition, they have no need for the tools and no medium in which to practise using them. Of course, we want our students to have mathematical computation skills. We want them to know how to construct grammatical sentences, to read accurately, to spell well, and to write neatly. The more automatic these operations become, the more students can focus on the real tasks in front of them.

Having these skills become automatic depends on practising them. The more writing students do, the less they have to stop and think which way round the *b* goes, or whether their sentences are grammatically correct. The more reading and writing they do, the more skill they are likely to have. Accuracy is the end product of much reading and writing, not a prerequisite for it.

And students cannot learn it before they do real reading and writing.

We used to say that children learn to read first, then read to learn. This makes as much sense as saying that children learn to talk first, then begin to communicate with other people. We cannot separate one activity from the other. First comes the purpose for talking or reading, then comes the gradual acquisition and refinement of the necessary skills.

We have to be very careful about cause and effect.

Once we discovered that children who read well sound out words well we jumped right in and drilled the phonics. Doing so didn't have the expected results. Of course a person who can read a word is good at sounding it out. It's sounding it out when we *don't* know what it is that's difficult.

We fell into the same trap with analytical grammar. People who are good language users and good writers tend to break down sentences into their component parts easily. Therefore, we thought, if we teach students how to analyze sentences, they will write better. It doesn't work, of course. They can only analyze language if they already know how it works, and if they know how it works, analyzing it is not going to teach them anything new.

If students don't know how language works, they need help in putting it together, not taking it apart.

This is where our modern gadgets can really help make learning easier. Take the word-processor, for example. It will not give a writer any help in composition. It will not tell anyone how to organize information. What it will do is take away some of the slug work of changing and recopying which can really get in the way of efforts to compose and organize. When I have thought up ways to make my writing better, it will make it easy for me to make the changes. Also, because the changes are easy to make, it gives a lot more incentive to try some improvements. If I can revise quickly and easily, I will do more of it. Once I am used to the idea that revision gives me a better product, unless I do it, I won't ever be satisfied. This is why writing never gets easier. The better we are, the harder it is.

Even before the mechanics of writing become automatic for students, they can benefit from technical help. Such help can enable them to focus on composition. Similarly, before computation becomes automatic, use of the calculator can allow students to focus on problem-solving and learn what math is really for. Listening to a story on tape can enable students to focus on content and reflect on meanings, without difficult print getting in the way.

An elderly woman once came up to me after I had talked to parents about teaching writing. She expressed concern that students these days were not expected to produce a perfectly neat final copy each time they wrote. She believed that finishing up with something that was less than perfect would not teach students true values. Leaving errors uncorrected was somehow a sign of moral weakness, or at best, laziness.

The woman did not understand that teaching is a lot like putting on a play. The students need plenty of rehearsal and coaching before what they are learning starts to come out right. We should regard much of what students do in school as early rehearsal: children are using and practising the new skills they are learning, but are not yet ready for a critical audience. We are looking at long-range goals.

I am not suggesting that students should not work hard, that we should shield them from failure, that they should expect success to come easily. Far from it. I want students to focus on what is really important.

We have already tried many ways to make learning easy for students. For example, for a while we reduced their reading to one-syllable-word gibberish with the well-intentioned view that they would find this easy. They gained a superficial accuracy, but did not really learn how reading is done.

We want to make learning easy for the students. This doesn't mean it always has to be fun, or broken down into little pieces, though. Everything doesn't have to be a game; I find that insulting to children. When children are engaged in a task they find meaningful, interesting and useful, they have attention spans at least as long as mine, sometimes longer, and they are prepared to work very hard. I saw my young students struggle at tasks which would have made me angry and frustrated in a fraction of the time.

Let us not be like the traditional generals, always fighting the last war. Let us rather take advantage of anything that can enable students to focus on the real tasks they need to learn and not get bogged down in a swamp of low-level skills. Let's get our priorities straight. After all, as Frank Smith once said, there is in the world a high correlation between cleanliness and literacy, but we can't teach anyone to read by giving them a bath.

Making It Real

Trying to trick children into learning by pretending it isn't work, but fun, is hypocritical. I do a lot of writing and take much satisfaction from it; I never regard it as fun. Only adults distinguish between work and play; for children, something is either worth doing or it is not. If we have to put up a sign to remind children that reading is fun, then something is lacking.

From birth, children have been struggling to find out about their world and to expand their horizons. Preschoolers are so intent on touching everything and exploring everywhere that sometimes a parent's main job is to keep them alive long enough to get to school. All children want to learn. Only when the tasks we give them lack real meaning do children cease to be motivated.

One thing that amazed me when I first worked in elementary schools was the way the children were taught to come into the building when the bell rang. The first two children held the door back for everyone else to go through. This job was much sought-after because these two children were the last to enter the school. They therefore had a legitimate excuse for arriving at their classrooms late.

This procedure allowed crowds of children to move efficiently through doorways, but did not bear much relationship to what goes on in the real world. The real skill of going through a door as a member of a group is to protect the nose of the person behind you. This skill does not seem to be taught or practised in school.

Many activities and procedures are just for school – they do not exist in the world outside. No real writer is judged on first-draft writing; writers, artists and artisans show only their best work to the public. Bookstores do not arrange their materials according to levels of difficulty, but in interest categories. The average adult never writes a book report. Nor do adults change tasks every 40 minutes, regardless of whether or not they have finished.

I used to know a teacher who got a job teaching in a large hospital where children stayed for extended periods. His classroom was the former drawing room of a large mansion. On moving in, he took the pictures down and arranged the desks so that the room looked more like a classroom and less like a home.

Today we are more sensitive to making the classroom inviting and accessible. Most of the teachers I know now do their best to make their classrooms comfortable, warm, and personal. They try to bring the real world in.

If we engage the children in real-life situations, then we can expect a real commitment from them. The more classroom activities reflect the real world, the more learning will take place.

Making It Last

In my early days as a history teacher, I can remember teaching a lesson about the Black Prince. I told the students all about young Edward, the epitome of mediaeval chivalry, winning glory in battles in France, and getting his name by winning the black armour of a defeated knight. I was at my storytelling best. For homework, I asked the students to write their own versions of the story of the Black Prince.

One girl wrote a most exciting story. She recounted every detail I had mentioned in the lesson, including the winning of the Black Knight's armour. There was just one problem. She had drawn a picture of the Black Prince in the famous armour – and had coloured it yellow.

But her account of the story was flawless. All the words she had written suggested that she understood the story completely. What had been in her mind as she coloured her picture? If I had known then what I know now – that what students do is less important in teaching than why they do it – I would have asked her. I probably just took off marks.

It wasn't until many years later that I recognized the significance of this incident. What she had gained from my lesson was only words, remembered long enough to complete the homework assignment. I wonder if she used these same short-term-memory methods to pass tests and exams. I wonder how long any of the learning lasted.

When I began school in the 1940s, schools hadn't changed much since education of the masses began in the late nineteenth century. Classwork was mostly memorization. We memorized the Bible, we memorized math facts and spelling rules, we memorized the important dates of history.* In my very first French lesson, we were given 20 vocabulary words for objects in the

---

* 55 BC, 1066, 1485, 1688, 1815, 1914. You can get a long way in British history with these.

classroom, and we had to memorize them for homework; the second lesson was a test. We spent much of our class-time chanting verb declensions. Science we learned by rote. The teacher performed experiments up at the front, while we watched. Our part was to write up the experiment. We had a formula for this; we wrote everything up under the same headings each time: Experiment, Apparatus, Method, Observations, Conclusion. I remember the formula – I remember none of the science.* When exam time came around we tried to memorize enough of the experiments to reproduce them on the test. If we were absent, we copied someone else's notes, and memorized them just the same.

I didn't realize, until I was faced with teaching math for the first time, that I didn't understand arithmetic. I could juggle numbers around the page and get the right answer enough of the time to get reasonable marks, but I did not understand the concepts I was dealing with. In school, I had memorized number tricks. I had not learned math concepts.

Our teaching is more effective today because in every subject we focus primarily on meaning. We focus on how the students respond, what they are taking away from the experience, and how they can use their learning. This is why, despite what we read in the newspapers, our students are better educated than ever before.

In our modern classrooms, we no longer value rote memorization. Learning is, by definition, understanding. If we understand, then we can learn to apply our knowledge in new situations. Only this kind of learning is useful; only this kind really lasts.

The basis for learning: **Meaning**
The purpose of learning: **Problem-solving**

---

* See the note on Miss Sawyer, page 87.

7

Teaching: What Works?

Direct Instruction or Exploratory Learning?

To one who doesn't know, it seems logical that the most efficient way to teach a lot of things to a lot of students is to sit them all down and teach them all at the same time. Teaching a point to a large group should be more time effective than teaching it individually, or to small groups. Unfortunately, it doesn't always work out this way.

I remember when I taught Grade 8, I used to teach the use of quotation marks. I knew I had to do this because the grammar textbook said so. November, I think. I used to provide lots of examples on the board, then assign the appropriate exercises in the book. Few of the students could do them. Those who could couldn't seem to use quotation marks in their own writing. Later on, as I worked my way down the age levels, I found I taught this same concept all the way down the line. Year after year we covered the material, and very few ever seemed to learn how to do it. Looking back, I see why. I was asking students to punctuate someone else's language, not their own; language they neither understood nor cared about. Just try reading someone else's dialogue without the quotation marks!

When I taught writing to Grade 1 students, I did much of my direct teaching as I was sitting down with a child in a conference. As soon as I saw any dialogue, I used to teach quotation marks. All I had to say was, "Someone is talking on your page; this is how we show that." They would put their hands around the part where someone was talking, and I would put in the quotation marks. Then I would invite them to go through the rest of the piece and fill in the others. Sometimes they did this by reading their piece aloud in the appropriate voices. They could all do it. After that, I made them responsible for this punctuation in their editing and found they could always do it. The teaching took about four minutes per child. These children will never need to learn this skill again. That individual teaching was time effective.*

Some kinds of information can be passed along through direct telling. If I want to pass on such a piece of information, I can certainly do this to a large group all at one time. I might describe how to write an address on an envelope, how the Black Prince got his name, or how to recognize a downy woodpecker. In these examples, the same information is appropriate for everyone. Some things we can learn by being told, particularly if we already know and understand something about the topic.

Other things we cannot learn by being told. We can't say we know how to make bread until we have got our hands in the dough and tasted the result. We can't learn to swim by reading about it. And you will only remember what I told you about the downy woodpecker if you care enough to go out and see one.

Some learning requires hands-on experience before we can understand it, and what we do not understand we will not remember. For example, we teach our young children to say "please" and "thank you" in appropriate places, but this is just stimulus-response activity: if they say "please," they get the cookie, and when they say "thank you," Dad is happy. They will learn the concepts of politeness, good manners and social convention through many life experiences and interaction with others.

The words behind the concepts carry no meaning in themselves. I have never met anyone who understands what *Good morning* means. We all learned the words, and when to say them, but we didn't learn what they mean. When someone says "Good morning" to you, that person is not commenting on the state of the day, but wishing for your well-being. So an appropriate response is, "Thank you," not "What's good about it?"

---

* I found it interesting that quotation marks seemed to be the first punctuation the children learned, and the easiest to teach them. After all, knowing when someone is talking on your page is easy; you need to understand the concept of sentence before you can put in periods, and clause before you can put in commas.

We have to decide which parts of our curriculum are points of information, and which are conceptual ideas. For points of information, go ahead and tell the whole class. But if you are expecting new understandings, don't waste your time.

In many cases, with the best will in the world, we feel we do not have time for the children to play, to explore, to experiment with materials, to make mistakes and have to start again. Also, the older students get, the more we seem to rely on telling, rather than hands-on experiences, and on whole-class teaching, rather than smaller groups. Critics of modern classrooms often propose that children spend less time playing and more time doing pencil-and-paper tasks. They don't understand that pencil-and-paper tasks represent experience only symbolically, that the experience must come before the symbols can be understood or used.

If we don't provide experiences, then concept learning will not take place, and we are wasting our time. We would do better to cut down on quantity and go for quality. After all, our job is not to find the quickest way to get through the material, but to find the best way, the one that will result in real and lasting learning.

> It is better to do something useful once a week than to do something useless every day.

Is Drill a Bad Thing?

During my second year of school, in Mrs. Small's class, we repeated the multiplication tables every morning. We also had whole-class chanting, counting by twos, by threes and by fives. It wasn't a dull chore; the rhythmic, singsong chanting was quite pleasant and familiar, not unlike the chanting we did in our own skipping rhymes on the playground. The repetition made these facts completely automatic for me, and I have always been grateful to Mrs. Small for that.

At one middle school, I taught next door to the geography teacher. Every year his Grade 7 classes memorized the countries of Africa. (I think there were 52 at that time.) When my homeroom class did this, they couldn't wait to come back and show me how well they could run through the whole African continent without forgetting one country. They enjoyed it as much as I enjoyed my number-chanting. But I wonder, how much use was it? For how long did the information even remain accurate?

This incident reminds me of another homework assignment from Miss Sawyer: to memorize the atomic numbers of the elements. We had them on a chart.* Even at the time, I didn't know what I was learning, or what use it could possibly be. Fortunately, the test was right after lunch, so I spent the whole lunch hour chanting the list. I was just able to get enough of the list down on the test to pass before I forgot it.

There's nothing wrong with memorization, with practice, with repetition. But drilling facts that the students do not understand the purpose of knowing and cannot use in their day-to-day work just wastes time. I would not want children to memorize multiplication tables until I was sure they understood the concept of multiplication, and had had plenty of opportunity to demonstrate their understanding with concrete materials. Once we understand a concept, then we can take shortcuts. If we do not understand what multiplication is, then even if we memorize all the tables, we cannot do anything with the information – we have wasted our time.

Making a few dummy runs is all right, as long as we get to do the real thing. We don't want them to spend all their time on the driving range and never get to the golf course.

Activity-centred Learning: Where We Fail

I was very proud of my activity-centred classrooms. I spent a long time choosing interesting topics and planning meaningful activities which would engage the children's attention. We were all busy, and we all had a good time. The industry and concentration of the children impressed me.

Now, as I look back, I can see the great weakness of what I was doing. I thought that when I had planned the activities and guided the children through them my job was done. I saw the activity as the end-product of teaching. I had subscribed to the view that if children are engaged in meaningful activities they will pick up the skills as they go along. Many children did, of

---

* There were 92 elements in those days. I think there are more than 100 now. I still don't know what they are or what they are for.

course. Some did not. For both groups, I was leaving learning to chance. I did not plan for it, could not monitor it, had no idea whether anyone had learned anything or not.

I failed to realize that the learning does not necessarily result from solving a problem, participating in a discussion, reading a story, or building a model. Learning centres on the thinking we do, both during and after the activity. Failure to accomplish a task can bring about learning, as long as we figure out what went wrong and have a better idea of what to do next time.

The problem was that I did not have a clear idea of the purpose of the activities I was planning. I thought that as long as students were reading, writing and talking, the activities must be good and productive. But creating activity in the classroom is not my goal; helping the students learn skills is.

The activity is my methodology. I use it because I know that children are more likely to learn language skills by using language to do things than by doing out-of-context exercises.

> Activity is a means of learning,
> not an end in itself.

Activity-centred Learning: How to Succeed

Here is an example of the way reflection can help learning. In my Grade 1 class I had been teaching the children about the concept of area. I don't know who decided that finding areas was an important skill for six-year-olds, but it was in the curriculum so I did it. The activities involved covering various surfaces with blocks or squares. After a couple of days of practice I asked the children to choose other surfaces to cover in this way. I gave them a recording sheet to write down what the surface was, what they had used, and how many it took to cover it.

Julie decided she would do the classroom floor.

I knew this was impossible. With 10-year-olds I would hope someone would figure out that they could count the floor tiles, but in Grade 1, I wouldn't expect this. However, I let Julie go ahead, watching to see what happened. She got a couple of friends to help her, and they started to cover the floor. After half an hour they had everything off the shelves, and the centre of the floor was a mess. They were so caught up in a frenzy of physical activity they did not think about what they were doing.

I knew I had to call a halt at some time, so I said to Julie, "It's almost recess, and no one can get out of the door. What do you think you ought to do?"

Then they stopped and looked. Two stages of shock registered clearly on their faces: first, the realization that they could not count all these objects; second, the more compelling thought that they would have to pick everything up and put it all away. The tears began to flow.

Then I had one of those rare insights which come in teaching, seemingly by accident, which prompt you to do just the right thing. I said to Julie, "We don't want anyone else to get into this mess. Why don't you write down what went wrong?" This is what she wrote:

It was difficult because we used small things.
You should use big things when you measure a big thing.
You should use small things when you measure a small thing

This represents one of the finest examples of concept learning I have ever seen. I had trouble teaching the notion of which unit to use in measuring to much older students, but here was a six-year-old who had made a discovery she would never forget.

Julie did not know she had made a conceptual leap. She knew only that she had made a mess and spent all morning clearing it up and had totally failed in her assigned task and looked a little foolish. But of the 31 children who worked on covering surfaces that week, Julie was probably the only one to learn a lasting lesson of real value. She would not have made this discovery had she not reflected on what she had done. The reflection might have been less complete had she not written down her conclusion. This incident shows the value of reflection through writing.

The other children had more activity, more hands-on experience, more feeling of success. But Julie was forced to ask herself the all-important questions that must accompany every activity, both in the classroom and in life: What does this experience mean? How does this relate to other facts I know? How can I use this new knowledge?

Focus is what matters. If I am going to plan for this reflective learning, rather than waiting for the rare occasions when it happens by accident, I must know what I want the students to get out of any activity I am planning for them. In other words, I must know which skills can be developed. Then I must build in time for reflection and help the students to focus on their learning. Here are a few ways to do that.

- At the end of a group activity, ask the group to talk for five minutes about their group processes: What worked well and helped you get the job done? Did anything make your job more difficult? If you had to do the activity again, what would you do differently?
- After a reading experience, either individual or group, ask questions that force students to compare, contrast, evaluate and make personal observations about what they have read.
- When you read a student's writing, ask questions, either personally or in writing, to generate reflection and explanation: "You didn't say much about _____. Was there a reason for this?" "I would be interested in knowing how you felt when _____ happened." "I don't understand what you mean here." "Why did you decide not to go on with this?"
- Use personal response journals to have students reflect through writing. Consider journals for all subjects across the curriculum. See a journal entry as a two- to five-minute response, not a lengthy writing assignment.

At first, ask specific questions to guide students' thinking: Which of the characters did you feel the most sympathy for? What did you find easy/difficult about doing this activity/project? What do you do when you want to write a word and you don't know the spelling? If a friend were going to do this study, what advice would you give to make it easier?

When the students are used to doing this kind of thinking, they will no longer need your prompts. With enough experience, reflection becomes a habit and a natural part of any activity, even when a journal is not used.

Many of us think that an activity-based program makes a classroom child-centred. We must not fall into the trap of thinking that activity is everything. Every activity must have purpose and focus, and we need to know the skills involved. If we know the skills we are trying to develop, then we can make sure they receive a focus at the appropriate time. We can also assess the children's learning of these skills and keep our notes and records accordingly.

> An activity is child-centred
> only if the child is learning from it.

8

Individualizing: How Much Do We Need?

Solitary Confinement

When I attended school, I never worked with a partner or in a group. Our only group was the whole class. We had to work alone on every task we were given; our teachers considered collaboration cheating and felt that it merited punishment and disgrace. They assumed that we would learn only if we thought everything out by ourselves. They assumed further that we could learn only from them and our textbooks; there was no place for discussion, for discovery, for helping one another. Also, every piece of work we did they assessed and marked, and totaled or averaged the marks to record our achievement and progress. We had to have a score that was ours alone. We spent our school life in a sort of solitary confinement.

One of the problems with this whole-class skills teaching of the past was that everyone received the same lessons and did the same exercises, at the same time, whether they needed them or not. Some of the students already knew the concepts and skills being taught, and so wasted their time. Other students lacked the awareness of language or sophistication of vocabulary to understand; they learned that language was difficult and complicated, something to avoid, if possible. Often they drew the conclusion that they read or wrote poorly and did as little of the activity as possible; their language development halted.

Another problem was that we taught many of the skills out of context. The students could not immediately use the spelling words, the grammar rules, and the punctuation marks in their own writing. Even if they remembered them, they could not apply them.

We wasted much of our classroom time. Because the skills had little to do with the students' real world, the study of language became irrelevant, repetitive and boring. But to learn a skill, we must practise it, as a doctor practises medicine – use it or lose it.

What we try to do now is identify what individual students need to know, and give help accordingly. But how can we do this when we have so many students to work with? And does this mean each student must have a different program?

We have tried to individualize programs through materials such as skill builders, skills labs, and more recently, computer programs. With many of these programs, students are placed at an appropriate skill level through a pre-test, then led through a sequence of activities and exercises at their own rate.

On the surface, this looks like individualization. Students work alone, each at a logically determined level. Progress is monitored through frequent checks. No one belongs to a low group. Students do not move on until they master current concepts. It all seems very organized and personalized.

However, many of the drawbacks of the old whole-class instruction are still present. All the students still perform the same tasks in the same way and study the same skills in the same order. None of the activities relate to their own writing, or to any topic or theme in progress. Customizing the activities or the content to match what the students need at any particular time is difficult. This kind of program results in another kind of solitary confinement in which students work blindly through a predetermined study sequence which may not bear their special needs in mind.

Conferences: Prime-time Teaching

One way we have tried to make our teaching individual is through the conference. When we sit down with a student and a piece of work in progress, we can find out what the student is trying to achieve, note the level of competence, and give the help and encouragement the student needs at the time he or she needs it. A conference provides an ideal way to make skills teaching relevant for each student and for each task. It is prime-time teaching.

The problem is, how do we find the time? Just how long can we spend with each student? How often can we sit down for uninterrupted time with one student? Is seeing the conference as the major vehicle for teaching skills really feasible?

Consider how many writing conferences you can do each day or in each writing period. If, for example, you teach only one class and you do five or six conferences, you have an opportunity to speak to each student once a week.* If you teach several classes and have a limited time for writing, you may be unable to speak with each student every week. If you do manage to talk to each student once a week, you are probably not spending more than six to eight minutes on each conference, which is usually plenty of time. (If you spend any longer than that, the child will forget most of what you have talked about before you get to the end.)

There is a suitable time for the teaching of every skill. We know we will not talk about spelling, punctuation or handwriting during first-draft writing or during the planning or organizing stages of the writing. We particularly do not want spelling to interfere with other, more important aspects of writing. Sometimes, students worry so much about spelling they can't focus on what they are writing about.

Most of the writing students do consists of early draft or exploratory writing, journal entries and notes, in which spelling and punctuation are not the primary concern. This means that in at least half the conferences you have with a student, you will not have an opportunity to mention spelling and other skills at all.

Let us suppose that at every second conference the purpose and stage of the writing will give you an opportunity to spend some time on skills. We probably won't spend the whole conference talking about skills; we will probably choose only one skills concept to talk about at a time, as even at late draft stages, many other aspects of writing must still be dealt with. Under this system, we will spend about three minutes every two weeks on skills. This adds up to 60 minutes of skills instruction for the whole year. In the old days we spent more time than this every week, and we have to think students remembered some of it.

---

* In workshops, I have asked thousands of teachers how many conferences they feel they can do each day. Most say two to four is the best they can manage. No one has ever claimed to do more than five or six on a regular basis.

Throughout the first six years of school, students might get the equivalent of one day's skills instruction. Even if we spend twice as much time as this – 12 conferences a day – can we really think it is enough?

How much of this kind of skills teaching can we plan for? How can we keep track of what we have taught, and to whom? Such incidental teaching usually turns out to be accidental teaching. Some children may get no skills teaching at all.

Some researchers recommend having a spelling conference, at which the total focus is spelling and other transcription skills. Having this would give a real opportunity to talk to a student about skills, to identify needs and to individualize instruction. But if we cannot find time for regular writing conferences, how will we find time for this? And how many times in a year would each student have this spelling conference? Would it be often enough to make a difference?

I consider writing conference time so valuable to the teaching of composition that I hate to see most of the time devoted to spelling and punctuation. Since spelling concepts and punctuation skills are common to everyone, they can often be handled in group sessions. Composition is unique to every writer and every piece of writing. We can help students in conceptualizing, organizing ideas and information, formulating language, and bringing a piece of writing to completion only one on one. I make this my priority for the small amount of conference time I have. I will spend what time I can on skills instruction, but this ranks at the bottom of my list of priorities.

I am not suggesting that we should not teach skills to individuals during conferences. Of course we should. For skills too, the conference is prime-time teaching, and we should do as much as we can. But we cannot count on teaching all skills on a one-to-one basis using each student's own writing. Given class sizes, that cannot be done.

Skills teaching through the individual conference is limited by more than logistics. It does not permit us to promote the discussion and negotiation that are part of group teaching and that contribute to group problem-solving. As part of a total skills package for my classroom, I want opportunities for my students to work together to collect and categorize words, to discover spelling patterns, to investigate language, to share strategies, to play word-games, to write according to predetermined formats and styles.

I want them to proofread together, not only so they can help one another, but so they can realize they share common problems. I also want times when I can give them information, initiate an investigation, demonstrate how a spelling rule works in practice, draw their attention to uses of language in their reading, and share anecdotes about the origins and history of words and sayings.

Individualization does not mean one-on-one teaching exclusively. This is impossible, given class sizes. It also limits the kinds of experiences we can provide for our students. We can better meet the needs of our students by using a combination of individual and group teaching methods.

Along with identifying the needs of our students, we must also pay attention to the requirements of the subjects and topics we are teaching. Some require an individual approach, while others suit a group experience better.*

Making the Most of a Conference

Conferences may allow us limited time with each student, but help given during a conference is personal and immediate. Very often, a few minutes spent in a conference can be just what a student needs to make a connection, learn a concept, or see how to proceed with a task. A conference is prime-time teaching for any aspect of writing, including skills.

There are two principles that can guide the choice of topic for a conference.
1. Match the topic to the stage of the writing. For example:
   First draft – content, information, ideas
   Later drafts – language use, word choice, organization
   Final draft – spelling, punctuation, handwriting, presentation
2. Choose one concept only for a teaching focus. For example:
   • Generation of more ideas
   • Addition of details to descriptions
   • Sorting of information into categories in order to build paragraphs
   • Choice of more effective verbs or adjectives
   • One aspect of sentence structure
   • One kind of punctuation mark
   • One word a student has misused or misspelt

---

* See the suggestions in chapter 7 on direct teaching and exploratory learning.

Group Teaching

Having a group of students, from two or three up to the whole class, work on the same topic can allow for a wide range of activities and experiences. Students can do the following:

- share strategies
- pool ideas
- play games and solve puzzles
- negotiate and discuss
- watch as you demonstrate
- listen as you explain
- proofread together
- collaborate on tasks that put skills to use

What we need is a judicious mixture of whole-class, small-group and individual teaching. We have to make decisions about which medium is the most suitable for each skill or topic we want to teach.

Individualizing does not mean we have to give each student different work to do. It does mean that when students share the same input and are given the same task, they produce work that is unique to each one of them. Each piece of writing is individual in purpose, in style, in content, in language and in presentation. Also, every piece of work serves as a window on a child's knowledge and ability as a user of language.

It is in the way we respond to the work students do that we individualize our teaching. We can base our assessment of a student's work and the help we give on what we know about that student's abilities, attitudes, and experience.

Skills in Context

We have a very real concern that skills be taught in context. Under the old methods, the skills we taught lacked any connection with other parts of our language programs. To counter that problem, more recently we have tried to teach skills through the children's writing. However, misconceptions about what *in context* means have left some holes in our teaching.

Context pertains to meaning and what we already know about topics we are reading or learning about. If we want to learn something new, we will find it easier to do if we can connect the new item with things we already know, with concepts we already understand. Recognition of the importance of context has led us to provide real literature for our children to read, not books with stilted, controlled vocabulary.

Children (and adults) find it harder to read non-fiction than fiction partly because they often do not have enough prior knowledge of the subjects they are reading about to understand and assimilate new knowledge. We usually find it helpful if children talk about a topic, share information, relate their own experiences, and use the vocabulary of a topic before reading about it. So if we want children to read a story about a mouse, we might talk about mice, look at some pictures, and share what we know about mice first. If we want children to learn to spell *mouse*, we won't put it in a list with *cheese* and *hole*.

Context and prior knowledge are equally important in skills teaching. We have to help the children see links and recognize patterns, so that they can make a spelling generalization. This generalization about a pattern and a structure enables the child to spell not only *mouse*, but other similar words in the future.

The learning of language skills depends largely on pattern recognition. A word is in a spelling context when it appears with other words that belong in the same spelling pattern. Seeing a group of words that all pertain to mice does not enable the learner to form any links and patterns.

Choosing some words from a student's writing to form a spelling list to study does not place the words in a spelling context. The only strategy the student has for learning the words is to memorize them individually – the most difficult and shortest-lived learning there is. The methodology fails to go beyond that in the old spelling textbooks.

In whatever subject we teach, we can plan our teaching around three kinds of grouping: whole-class, small-group, and individual conference. If, in our teaching, we try to put all our focus and energy into only one of these methods, then we are missing many opportunities. Using all three kinds of teaching widens our range of strategies, improving our chances of accommodating different learning styles and of engaging every student.

Skills become individualized when students use them successfully to accomplish their own purposes.

9

Structure: Who Needs It?

The Non-structured Classroom

When I first began teaching, I thought that being a good teacher meant such things as having an always-quiet class, giving a sparkling performance up at the blackboard, correcting assignments promptly, and efficiently keeping a book full of marks to be averaged at report time. In those days, I wanted to have the students' full attention on me at all times. I wanted to be in complete control. The teachers I envied and attempted to emulate were the ones who commanded instant obedience, had silent classrooms, left stacks of neat notebooks around the staffroom, and knew how to use the copying machine.

Later on, my priorities changed. I had discovered that learning was something the students had to *do*, not something I told them about. What I wanted then was an active classroom, the students self-motivated, with ownership of and investment in the work they were doing.

In my last classroom, I used low walls to divide the space into different work areas.* The children often worked on many different things, sometimes by themselves, sometimes with other children, sometimes with me. They had certain tasks and assignments they were expected to work on, but they planned much of their own time, spent the time they needed for each job, then moved

---

* I built the walls with four ft. by eight ft. sheets of softboard held up with a row of desks on either side. They not only gave privacy, but a lot more space to display the children's work. Note: Always tell the school secretary about what to expect before having the lumberyard deliver.

on to the next one. There was movement and talk, and few house-keeping instructions from me.

Visitors invariably referred to this as a "non-structured" class-room. This label really annoyed me, because I had taken years to evolve a way of organizing and managing this kind of program so that real work got done. This classroom had far more under-lying structure than the time-table dominated, textbook-dependent, teacher-directed classrooms I used to run.

In this new kind of classroom, I knew that the students and I had to share decision-making; the students had to control part of what went on during the day. How dangerous! What if they didn't learn everything they were supposed to? What if they didn't do things the right way? How would they learn if I didn't teach them everything?

I found the management questions even more pressing. Would I lose control? What would other teachers think of me if my students made a lot of noise? How would I keep track, if everyone wasn't doing identical work? However would I write my planbook?

A Balancing Act

I had to deal with the question, Who is doing the structuring? I had to decide on the kinds of experiences I wanted my students to have. What did I want them to do? Then I had to decide which of these activities I needed to control and which could best be left to the students. Professional literature often describes this process as *negotiating the curriculum*. The result is a balance between teacher direction and student control.

This process provides a vehicle for helping students learn how to initiate and plan their own learning, organize their time, and make reasonable choices. It also recognizes that we must main-tain a balance so that we can control the overall content of the curriculum and ensure that our students are exposed to a wide range of experiences and skills.

Consider that a major aim of education is to produce students who can continue to learn after they have left school. Schooling consists of more than accumulating facts; that we can do by play-ing Trivial Pursuit. We can no longer make a list of things a per-son needs to know to get on in life. I'm not sure we ever could, although I remember one parent who came to my classroom after school demanding to know why I had not yet taught his son to memorize the names of the counties of Ontario;* he had done it when he was in Grade 7. How many of these kinds of facts that we learned in school can we still remember? We all recognize that remembering them doesn't matter; it's not what was important. Regurgitating a collection of facts does not mark an educated person.

So much of what we do in everyday life, both at work and at home, involves planning, organizing, and carrying through a series of tasks. Someone once drew a distinction between those who work hard and those who work smart. I guess those who work both hard and smart have really got something.

We know that education must enable us to solve new problems, to evaluate new information, to find answers to our own questions. Therefore, giving our students practice in planning and organizing their own learning makes as much sense as giving them practice in reading or math.

What makes no sense is to take those students who cannot organize themselves, and do the organizing for them. The ones we say need more teacher direction, or a more structured program, really need the most help in doing without it. After all, I don't identify those who can't do math and then do it for them. I can't think of anything we learn better by having someone else do it for us. Certainly, reducing tasks to manageable proportions, providing models and patterns, and suggesting solutions to problems can help. Human nature encourages us to let someone else do things for us whenever possible – none of us really learned to look after ourselves until we were out in the world on our own. But ultimately, every student will have to rely on his or her own resources.

Students who plan their own learning will get into a mess some of the time. When they are first starting, they will fail a lot of the time. I have to expect this and allow it to happen. The students can only learn to make good decisions through experience. If they are going to learn from their mistakes and failures, they need to reflect on their experiences, evaluate their performance, and plan new strategies to try next time. They do not need to have responsibility taken away from them.

---

* As a fairly recent immigrant, I had not yet realized that Ontario even had counties.

The problem is, when our classrooms get into a muddle and things don't work out right, we see it as a reflection on our own abilities. We still have the notion that a successful teacher has a smoothly running classroom, orderly students and complete control. We can't help wondering what other teachers will think of us.

Isn't learning how to structure our own learning one of the most important things we can learn in school? Do you remember the panic in taking university courses, when you were given no clear direction about topics for study or length or style of assignments and had to make your own choices? Life is so much easier when someone else makes these kinds of decisions for us. I have to remember, though, that I will not always be there; my students need the ability to organize and plan for themselves.

A non-structured classroom cannot survive. A question of balance, of negotiation between teacher and students, governs the nature of a classroom. The teacher must be responsible for the overall structure of what is studied and how. Within that structure, the students can have a range of choices, both in the content and in the study methods. In this way, the teacher can guide in the right direction, while allowing students room to devise their own best ways of working.

Often I hear about children who "need more structure." Sometimes this comment applies to whole-class or school populations. It refers to children who seem to waste their time and never get anything finished, who have short attention spans, who fool around a lot and disrupt the class. These children seem to take up more of our time than those who quietly get on with their work. You may have heard about the teacher who was asked what was the perfect class size. He replied, "Three less than I have – and I can name the three!"

One thing that we teachers find difficult to handle is children wasting time and not getting their work done. We feel we must step in immediately and give the children a regimented day with little room for flexibility. Making our classrooms more teacher-directed can make for short-term gains in the amount of work that is finished and in the orderliness of our rooms.

Short-term gain, however, is not what we are after in school. We care about what the student will take away on leaving our class, our school, our education system. What kind of future are we preparing our children for if we allow them to depend on someone else to organize and plan their every move? Many jobs, certainly all of the more interesting ones, demand that the worker be able to plan and organize time and resources. The worker must also be able to accept responsibility for getting the job done on time. In their leisure time, will our students sit around and wait for television to entertain them, or will they have the independence to plan for and follow through on participating in more challenging pastimes? The people who handle retirement the worst are those who, once the discipline of their job is taken away, cannot find satisfying ways to structure their own time.

All learning must have structure to be successful. Even if we work by trial and error, we must be organized, so we don't waste time repeating the errors. We need to consider who does the structuring. If I don't establish exactly when the children will read and how long they will take, that doesn't mean my classroom lacks structure. It just means that the children will do the structuring, not me. If there is no structure, the reading will not get done.

We sometimes fear that children won't know what to write about unless we tell them, won't read unless we make them accountable afterwards, won't read anything worthwhile unless we choose it for them. The first time we throw them back on their own resources, this may well be the case.

When I started independent reading with Grade 7 students, they read the shortest and easiest books they could find. They also tested my assertion that they could read anything they liked by bringing in biker magazines and comic books. I had to let them work through this until they believed that they had real choice and then became bored enough to choose more challenging and interesting material. I exercised a kind of subversive control by doing book-promotion talks, reading aloud some exciting excerpts, having good books there for them to browse through – and spending more time talking with students reading interesting books.

Similarly, when they began doing personal writing and I provided no topics, some of them sat for days and produced next to nothing; others wrote about the same thing over and over again. I talked to them and tried to stir up their interest in topics they knew a lot about. Sometimes, I paired them up to generate ideas together. I was weaning them from what Lucy Calkins calls *Writers' Welfare*, the system that keeps children dependent on the teacher for handouts of topics to write about.

We must not give up too quickly when students fail to organize themselves, and the learning we have planned for does not materialize. Self-discipline is the hardest kind to learn, and none of us can become skilled overnight. Achieving self-discipline takes constant practice, and like everything else, we must keep on trying, knowing that we can expect to get better as we go along.

Even when a student fails to produce anything, I must not step in and take over responsibility. I must provide as many opportunities as I can in the classroom for students to initiate their own learning, organize their own time, manage their own materials, and reflect on their own performance. At each of these stages, I can help, and so can other students, but the student must take the ultimate responsibility.

Learning demands self-motivation, as well as an ability to organize in order to accomplish tasks and solve problems. Just as self-motivation is tied to skills of meaning, problem-solving is tied to skills of process. (See chapter 5.) Expecting to make progress with skills of content alone just wastes time.

Sometimes we feel the pressure of curriculum weighing down on us. We feel that, if we give students the luxury of time for experimenting, for following their own interests, for failing, we will not get through the content of the curriculum or course of study.

We must not bend to this tyranny. Let us not make the curriculum a meat grinder through which to squeeze our students. Trying to fast-track our students through the curriculum would likely teach many of them that learning is difficult and boring; we won't produce self-motivated and competent learners that way. We must insist on a reasonable amount of real and lasting learning, not a superficial process of going through the motions. As Murphy's Law states, and any driver can attest, a shortcut is the longest distance between two points.

Taking Risks

The classroom has to be a place where things go wrong, not a place in which everything looks perfectly efficient and organized. If things aren't going wrong much of the time, then the students are not taking many risks, and we know that learning requires risk-taking. The same thing applies to us. If we are not going wrong some of the time, then we are not taking risks either. How can we help other people learn if we are not learning ourselves? How else can we understand how learning works, and gain insights about what helps and what hinders?

How do we teach students that being wrong can be a good thing? Trying something out and later deciding to abandon it as a bad idea can be a productive strategy. Most students, and many of their parents, though, believe without questioning that getting everything right all the time ranks above everything else and indicates success in school. This is the tyranny of marks and grades.

Consider that we all learned to talk by taking risks constantly. For several years we spoke imperfectly nearly all the time. Our parents, though, rewarded our efforts, focused only on our successes, and never penalized us for being incorrect. Can you imagine a parent describing a two-year-old as a B+ in talking, a C in listening, and a little below average in walking?

When do children learn that taking risks is dangerous? Students must understand that any learning needs risk-taking; therefore, we must show them that we value experimentation and innovation, that we see failures as signs that they are trying out new ideas and techniques, that we care about whether they are getting closer to success, not just that they are achieving it.

Encouraging the taking of risks must affect our evaluation policies. Anytime a student feels penalized for making a mistake, that student will see risk-taking as dangerous and will avoid it. If making a spelling mistake results in a lot of extra work or loss of marks, that student will always write *big*, never try *enormous*. So we must do much of our evaluation of student performance covertly. We should not make students accountable and on record for everything they do in the classroom.

Summative evaluation should reflect only their best work, not everything they do. After all, in the real world, we assess the worth of artists and artisans on their best work, that which is published or displayed, not on everything they have ever produced. Who knows what Hemingway put in the garbage can? Students should be able to wipe their failures from the record too. We should see most of what they do in school as practice and experiment, not performance subject to evaluation.

We have to find that fine line which allows us to reward risk-taking and accept failure, while still maintaining the value of excellence and achievement.

Doing this means letting the students in on the learning process. They should know, for example, that with first-draft writing, they should experiment, they should try things out. Failing first-draft writing is impossible, unless they write nothing at all. Donald Graves said that writing can never be wrong – just unfinished. The idea of marking first-draft writing, the experimental stage of writing, is ludicrous. On the other hand, before a student makes a piece of writing public, mails the letter or shares the story, that student must work on the writing until it is the best product possible. At this point, the writer should expect some kind of audience reaction, and be prepared for criticism.

If the writer understands when risk-taking is desirable and when form and accuracy are important, then the writing is more likely to succeed. Similarly, in our recreational reading, we can take huge risks with meaning, skipping large chunks, reading quickly, filling in the blanks from our own prior knowledge. But if we do this with recipes and maps, we are likely to get into trouble.

A Practical Model

Here's how a balanced, child-centred classroom can work in practical terms.

In the reading program, there will be part of the day when I will select literature, decide how the students will experience it, lead discussion, initiate group inquiry, perhaps plan for some kind of response activity. I can thereby widen the students' experience of literature, help them look for deeper meanings, enable them to access literature they might be unable to read alone, create situations for group interaction, demonstrate how a reader wrestles with a text. I am mostly teaching process skills here – how to go about the task.

There will be another part of the day when the students will choose their own reading materials. Doing this allows them to follow their own interests, read at a level of difficulty they feel comfortable with, go at their own pace, learn to make choices, find their way around the library, get into a reading habit. When they are alone with a text, they can practise in a real way the skills of reading I have helped them learn in my half of the program.

Similarly in writing, students will spend part of the program on personal writing. They will each choose their own topics, decide on format and style, make decisions about revision and presentation. I will work with them, through their writing conferences, to provide initial audience reaction, to help them develop their topics, and to teach them specific skills as they need them; in general, I will take whatever they are trying to do, and help them do it better.

This personal writing, however, will not necessarily give the students a chance to experience all the different kinds of writing. We know that writing a poem differs greatly from writing instructions, composing a story, making notes, formulating a business letter, or keeping records.

Therefore, I will assign specific writing tasks. In this way I can ensure that the students write in different modes and for different purposes. They may write in a personal, expressive way in response to literature they have read, learn the specialized formats needed for information-bearing writing, and create literature of their own to share with classmates. We also know that writing does more than show what we know; it provides an important way of learning. I will want my students to use exploratory writing across the curriculum as a part of the learning process.

This means that at times all my students will share in the same reading or writing experience. These are the times for me to take the lead, to determine which skills I want to focus on, to structure both the input I provide and the response the students will make. Within this framework, each student will respond in a personal way, according to his or her interest and ability.

At other times, the students will make individual choices about what to read and write about. I remain involved. I help with the choices, talk about the reading and ask just the right questions to get the students thinking more deeply, and talk about the writing, showing an interest, keeping the students moving forward, and helping to solve immediate problems.

Whenever I feel I need to step in to steer a student, I can take over more of the control in subtle ways. For example:

• If a student has begun several pieces of writing, but not finished anything, I can say, "Which of these stories are you going to finish?" That is better than saying, "Are you going to finish one of these?" The student remains in control, but I have limited the options.

- When I talk to children about their writing, I often find that they tell me many details they did not include in the writing. I won't say, "Are you going to put that into your story?" A far better question is, "Where in your story do you think that could fit?" Then I can demonstrate how to write the information at the bottom of the page and put an arrow showing where it is to go. I will have taught revision and an editing shortcut in one easy step. The student remains in control, but again I have limited the choices. I have not left the child the option of choosing "No."

Being child-centred does not mean letting the children think that all the decisions they make are right. Nor does it ever mean that children have the right to choose whether to work or not. Allowing children to make choices and take on responsibility differs from letting them do as they like. Also, I do not have to accept and praise all their decisions. When students go in the wrong direction, I need to tell them about it, and help them find a better way next time.

I have always thought it interesting that five-year-olds can make choices, choose their own activities, handle their materials, and learn classroom routines very quickly. Their classrooms reflect a desirable balance between teacher control and student choice. Why can't we continue this as the children grow older?

The real basic skills
motivating oneself
making informed choices

10

Textbooks: Do They Have A Place?

Textbook Tyranny

When I came to Canada, after five years teaching secondary-school history with field hockey three afternoons a week, I was assigned to teach two classes of 11-year-olds as a home-room teacher. This meant I taught English, Math, History and Geography to one class in the morning and to another in the afternoon.

The English divided up as reading comprehension, spelling, grammar and creative writing. Another teacher taught something called Literature, while a third did Drama. I did not know what these other two teachers did, and it never occurred to me to ask. We didn't ask questions in those days. We tried to give the impression that we knew everything.*

I understood my responsibilities clearly. The textbooks that I had set them out. I had a Speller with weekly lists for the students to learn and work prescribed for each day. All I had to do was read out the list for the test on Friday. I had a set of skill builders and a reading lab, both of which required the students to read a short passage and answer comprehension questions. Following my secondary-school training, I made sure I kept records of the scores for each student. I also had a grammar text, so we had a verb week, a comma week, and so on until we

---

* One of the healthiest developments I have seen in my teaching life has been the way we now talk to one another, and share with one another – not only our successes, but our problems. Collaboration works for us, as well as for the children.

covered all aspects. The students did the exercises from the book, and I kept records of the marks.

Every Thursday at 2 p.m. I taught creative writing. I didn't have a textbook for this. I wracked my brains to come up with three enticing topic choices each week. The only topic I can remember is "My Life as a Centennial Dime." (It was 1967.) I remember this one because the superintendent came in to evaluate me, and to get myself out of a tricky situation, I had the students take turns to read their stories aloud. He congratulated me on my choice of topic.*

Teaching was easy in those days. The textbook provided all the information. Sometimes we would have the students take turns to read aloud from the book, or if we wanted some variety, we let them read silently. (The fast readers always had to wait for the slow ones to finish. Because this caused a discipline problem, we would start asking the questions before the really slow ones were ready.) The manuals told us what questions to ask and what answers we should get. I focused mainly on crowd control, making sure the students kept to their tasks and did not talk to one another.

Planning was easy, too. I started on page one of each of the textbooks and gradually worked my way through them. Good long-range planning we equated with getting to the end of the book at the end of June. My Day Book showed a series of page numbers written in time slots; this way I could assure myself that I was covering everything. I looked forward to the day when I could get my Day Book in good enough shape to laminate it the way the older teachers did.**

Such textbook-bound teaching is what we have all been trying to get away from in the past 25 years. It brought along with it three-group reading, marks and scores. It dominated not only the curriculum but also our evaluation and reporting. The year I spent teaching this program was orderly, but boring. I can't imagine what any of the students got out of it. It would only reinforce any notion they had about the irrelevance of school to their lives.

---

* This same superintendent gave me an *A* for windows (the blinds were all pulled down equally) and a "neatly recorded" for register. He wrote on the report, "The classroom is no place for laughter."

** I learned all about Day Books during my first two months in Canada. When I arrived in the classroom as a supply teacher, I had only to locate the page numbers in the appropriate textbooks and the children could work. Leaving the day's work uncorrected was the worst crime a supply teacher could commit.

Textbook Sense

In our efforts to escape the textbook tyranny of the past, we have gone from one extreme to the other. We now tend to regard any activity prescribed in a book as bad. Because our students used to spend so much time working through duplicated sheets of activities and questions, we now regard all workbooks as inappropriate and outdated.

Perhaps we mistrust textbooks and workbooks because they come in sets and enable a group of students to read and study the same subject at the same time. We have been told that such uniformity is wrong and not in keeping with modern teaching philosophies. Also, we want to reserve the right to design our own units of study; we don't necessarily want to follow those set out by the authors of a textbook. Exercising this right places tremendous demands on teachers, especially in elementary schools where we cannot be experts in every subject we have to teach.

Of course, we all want to teach with spontaneity, teaching in our own way, following the students' interests, allowing for individual differences.

Doing without a textbook is fine, as long as we fill the gap with something better. When we abandoned the old Spellers, we did not know how else to handle spelling instruction. We either left spelling to chance, or we replicated the methodology of the old Spellers by making new word-lists from the children's writing. When we stopped using Readers, we provided good reading material, but often ignored or overlooked the skills teaching.

There seems to be a feeling that if we assign activities from a book, we are showing weakness, laziness or ignorance. Given the limited time we have to plan for our students, this perception is unfair. Many teachers bought sets of literature anthologies for their classrooms but consultants actively discouraged them from buying the accompanying Teacher's Manuals. Old Readers had manuals with low-level questions and busywork activities, so newer versions were dismissed out of hand, without an evaluation of their contents. That left teachers without support for the literature they were using, and without the time to develop worthwhile activities of their own. Many of us lacked the experience to know how to get the maximum teaching potential from a story and lost opportunities to teach skills in a meaningful way.

To dismiss textbooks out of hand as "all bad" is irresponsible. An article is just as true if printed in a textbook rather than in a library book. Publishing a story in a student anthology rather than bound in its own cover does not diminish the story's worth. A textbook can make both the article and the story more accessible to the student if it places them in a context with other related material and suggests ways students can respond to and learn from the reading. Consequently, the article and the story become more useful both to the teacher and to the student.

An activity can be just as relevant when it comes from a Teacher's Manual as when it comes directly from the teacher. If someone more expert in the field than I am has devised the activity, it can be considerably better. As the teacher, I can pick and choose from the activities suggested. We are quite capable of evaluating the content of a book or the nature of an activity and of deciding whether our students would find it useful.

What is wrong with a group of students, even as large as the whole class, using the same book at the same time? How does this differ from me reading a story to the whole class? My informed selection of the material to be used, as well as the way in which I have each student access the material, makes an activity or experience child-centred. The way each student uses the information received and the way I respond to what each one does make the activity individual.

Nothing is wrong with the concept of a textbook. It is the content and how it is used that count. However, we need a new kind of textbook, and we need a more balanced and rational view of how we can use such resources to our advantage.

First, a textbook should serve as a resource, rather than provide a predetermined series of sequenced lessons. We read fiction and non-fiction differently. Fiction we usually read more or less sequentially from beginning to end, while non-fiction we may dip into as needed. A text should allow for flexible use; it should not demand that we return to the lockstep routine of everyone working through everything from beginning to end.

Having multiple copies of a book can provide us with fresh teaching opportunities. We can teach students how to read non-fiction, how to choose information, how to make notes as they go, how to combine information and opinion from different sources. I can't remember ever giving students much help with any of these before sending them off to the library to do research.

Teaching these skills individually through each student's own research and writing is a wonderful idea, but how can we find the time? We risk falling into the accidental and haphazard teaching I talked about in chapter 8. If we do, students may never learn the skills. No wonder my students always came back from the library with the encyclopedia copied out.

Secondly, we need to use textbook resources intelligently. There are many advantages in having a group of students, sometimes even a whole class, read the same thing at the same time. A classroom rarely has every single student engaged on a different course of study. And surely in math, history, geography or science, we want the students to learn a basic body of knowledge.

My students would have learned a lot more science if I had had a textbook, written by experts in science teaching, to refer to and adapt to my needs.

A workbook, textbook or manual that engages a student's interest, provides relevant information, stimulates interaction, prompts thinking, and inspires further study can be just as child-centred as an activity I plan myself. A well conceived and written book may be more so.

The most important reason we value literacy so highly is that it gives us access to the collective knowledge, insight and wisdom of the world. It seems ironic that we have largely removed books as a medium through which our children can learn in the classroom.

> There is nothing wrong with the **concept**.
> It is the **content** we need to evaluate.

11

The Classroom: What Should It Look Like?

A Teacher-centred Place

When I was a child in school, we considered getting a desk of our own a sign of growing up. We started out with two-seaters, first with a fixed lid, then in the second year with a double lift-up lid. We sat in boy-girl pairs; I think the idea was that the boys and girls would have little to do with each other. When we went to high school, we got individual desks with unattached seats. We knew we had graduated from childhood into adulthood.

The first classroom I taught in was the most beautiful I have ever had. A corner room, it had two walls all glass. From one window I could see the playing fields and surrounding trees; from the other I could see the front driveway, and keep track of everyone coming and going. I positioned the desks so that the students had their backs to the windows. Only I faced outwards.

My classroom arrangement showed what I felt was important. The students were to focus on me, not on the outside world. The desks stood in rows so every student was alone. The desks all faced the front; students were supposed to interact only with me – never with one another. One glance established that here was a teacher-centred place.

I remember when activity centres first began to appear in classrooms. Teachers typically set them up on tables and desks around the outside of the room, while ranging the children's desks in the middle. The children could go to the centres after they finished their other work. Slower students often never got to the centres at all.

What kind of statement did this make about what was central and what was peripheral? If we believed that working at the centres brought about learning better, shouldn't this have been the "real work"? What kinds of conclusions did the children draw about what was really important?

No rules govern what a child-centred classroom ought to look like. However, certain kinds of arrangement make better statements than the one I made with that first classroom.

A Child-centred Place

Trauma hit when we first began to get our desks out of rows and put them into groups. The biggest problem was with the cleaning-staff – cleaning takes a lot longer when the broom does not slip easily between rows. We would come in on Monday morning to find that the cleaning-staff had put all the desks back into rows. It used to take some time before the students could find which desk was theirs. We then defiantly put the desks back into groups for another week.

For a while, we were in an intermediary stage between teacher-centred and child-centred – we were janitor-centred.

For a time, school planners believed that open-plan schools were more child-centred. We had schools with few interior walls, where six or eight classes operated in the same space, and often shared some facilities, like sinks and art areas. We were trying to avoid pigeon-holing children and trying to promote a more flexible movement of children between classes and teachers. We sought to physically break the barriers between age levels and see the children as individuals rather than as grade-level statistics.

Yet when you walked through these areas, you were aware of the invisible walls. Teachers spent all day saying, "Sh!" No one could do drama at all, and music posed a real problem. The wide-open spaces inhibited children and teachers more than they liberated them.

When I became a consultant, I had the experience of working in an open-plan office, rather like these open-plan schools. I found it impossible to work in this environment due to lack of privacy, peace and quiet. Whenever we had a meeting, we went into an enclosed meeting room. Whenever we had to concentrate on writing, we took it home. So when I returned to the classroom, in my attempts to make a child-centred place, I aimed for exactly the opposite of open plan. I wanted the children, also, to be able to go into a meeting room for some privacy. I built walls.*

To be child-centred, a room must accommodate many different learning and teaching styles. There should be a place for the whole class to work together, a place for small groups to meet without disturbing anyone else, and a place to work alone in privacy, peace and quiet.

The way a room is organized can affect the quality of the activities that take place in it. Anyone who has done workshops will tell you this. When a small group of people is spread thinly around a large room, there is no contact, no interaction. Everyone is reserved and quiet. But when people sit close to one another a group spirit develops. People become participants, rather than spectators. Speakers know this. That is why they are upset when the audience sits at the back. Establishing any kind of rapport will be very difficult, if not impossible, and both audience and speaker will go away feeling less satisfied.**

A classroom can also be more child-centred if materials are accessible to the students. If all the supplies – paper, scissors, hole-punches, books, and so on – are available, and the children are made responsible for their care and use, then children have ownership in the room.

A classroom should also reflect student input.

I used to pause sometimes when I was spending time in school during holidays and in the evenings making beautiful bulletin boards, and ask myself, "Who am I doing this for?"

I never particularly noticed that the children paid much attention to what I had done. I suspect I did it to impress the other teachers and to meet the unwritten rule that bulletin boards had to be covered with coloured paper. I used to put up student writing, but no child ever went up to read it. In my early days in Canada, I had a principal who bought me a book on bulletin boards. He obviously thought mine were lacking in something, although he was too polite to say so.

Later on I had a better rule for myself: never do anything in

---

* See the footnote on page 68.
** I have often wondered why people come early for a workshop to make sure they get bad seats at the back where they will be unable to see or hear so . well. What are they afraid of? Do they want to be spectators, not participants? It seems to be a principle that the older the students taught, the more likely the teacher is to sit at the back.

the classroom that a student can do. So I gave over the bulletin boards to my students. The result was a real mess a lot of the time. They could never get things straight, and they didn't understand about borders and frames. No one ever glanced into my room and raved over the bulletin boards – except the students. I could have saved myself a lot of work if I had realized before that what mattered was not that the board was perfect, but that it was theirs.

The room must be warm and inviting, a place that reflects the students who spend time in it. I always find it striking that when I go into a high-school classroom the walls are usually bare, showing no sign that students have ever been there.

A child-centred room may not look picture-perfect, but in it children know that they are central.

In a child-centred classroom,
children are not visitors in the teacher's office,
but residents of their own.

12

Evaluation: How Do We Keep Track?

Making It Meaningful

I remember the first mark I got in high school in England. I was 11 years old, very small and shy, and already confused as a result of getting lost on the way to Science. As I arrived, Miss Sawyer* was handing back the first homework assignment. This was the typical science homework – to write up the experiment we had seen the teacher do at the front of the class – and it didn't vary much during the next several years. As she called names and handed out the papers, Miss Sawyer threw in suitable comments, so that everyone in the class knew what mark you had, and what stupid errors you had committed. When she got to mine, she said, ''C. That wasn't very good, was it?''

I had no idea what she meant. In my little three-room primary school we had always been given marks out of 10. At least I picked up that *C* meant my work had not impressed her. I found out in time that she docked marks if you didn't use a 2H pencil for the diagrams. That was the same Miss Sawyer who, a couple of years later at a parent interview, told my mother I was ''pretty mediocre.'' I give my mother a lot of credit for bursting out laughing.

Then there was Miss Francis, the Latin teacher. In four years of trying, I never discovered the secret of Latin translation, let alone the purpose of it, even though, to Miss Francis, it was

---

* I have mentioned Miss Sawyer several times in this book. Science was the only subject I failed in school; I wonder why I have so many memories of Miss Sawyer's class?

clearly filled with supreme joy and fascination. I was amazed when, on one report, she wrote that my syntax was improving. I had been teaching for 10 years before I found out what syntax was. It wasn't often my teacher told me I was improving in Latin. I found it hard to continue improving when I didn't know what I had done right.

Another highlight of my evaluation memories was the time a friend and I did our French homework together. Susan was an A+ student in every subject. She later won a handful of scholarships to Cambridge and achieved such high marks that the board of governors gave the whole school icecream cones and a half-day holiday to celebrate. After a weekend spent at my house, Susan and I handed in word-for-word identical translations. (Doing so was pretty safe – we were three-quarters of the alphabet apart.) She got an *A*; I got a *B+*. And my handwriting was as good as hers, if not better. Miss Campbell obviously saw her as an A and me as a B+. Inevitably, so did I.

Miss Saunders, the games mistress, provided another highlight. She had been complaining that not enough people tried out for the netball team. I didn't think much of netball, preferring games like lacrosse and tennis, which allowed you to wield a weapon, but I took her pep-talk to heart. I was very good at sports in school and in a fervour of school spirit, I turned out for the next netball practice. After the session, Miss Saunders told me not to bother coming back. Her exact words in evaluation of my efforts were, "You're not much use to me, are you?" It was two years before anyone could persuade me to try out for a school team again.

I remember only one comment the English teacher ever wrote on my writing. Not only do I remember the comment, I remember exactly what I had written that she liked so much. We had to write a composition, no kidding, about what we had done on the summer holiday. I wrote about a day my family had spent in the New Forest. I used the phrase, "Out came bats and balls." She wrote in the margin, "nice." I thought it was nice, too. I got *B+*.*

Three times a year came the reports. Every teacher put a term mark, an exam mark, and a one-line comment. The one-liners showed little originality: "could do better," "generally satis-

---

* I cannot remember the name of this teacher, although she taught me English for seven years, and I can picture her clearly and still hear her voice declaiming Wordsworth. Do we recollect bad experiences more easily?

factory," "exam result disappointing," that kind of thing. I always got "good" for games and gym, the only goods I could count on. I didn't have to wait for Miss Humm's assessment to know I could do that.

Once we had been evaluated, we weren't expected to do much about it. Unless we got a *D*, that is. If our work was really terrible, we got a *D* and had to stay for detention and do the work again. Getting a *D* was a big disgrace. My only experience in school of having a second try at a piece of writing came this way; doing a second draft was a punishment, something to be avoided at all costs! This kind of evaluation taught me that a good writer gets everything perfect in one try. My teachers were not telling me the truth.

Looking back as a teacher on my own schooling, I know that the education I received was fine. My teachers knew how to create a climate for learning and for personal growth. They encouraged us to ask questions, to make our own judgments, to express our own opinions, to initiate our own investigations, to be responsible for ourselves. We learned concepts, not just facts. A generation before the term appeared in professional literature, we had ownership of our own learning.

I wonder, though, how the evaluation practices contributed to the learning process. Every piece of work I did was solely for the purpose of evaluation. We never had a chance to experiment, to try something new. The only feedback came from the teacher, and that was always well after we had finished our work. There was no other audience, no other purpose. The evaluation rarely told me specifically what I had done well, or what I should do to become better. Anyway, by the time I received it, the piece of work was history; there was little point in working on it any more. I was judged, not helped. It seemed we learned for the purpose of answering the questions on exams. We even practised writing answers to exam questions, to make sure we would know the right way to do it.

In retrospect, I think the evaluation practices I experienced worked against what my teachers wanted me to learn. Learning involves taking risks, failing much of the time, practising and practising before we get things right, but gradually getting closer and closer to where we want to be. Motivation to learn depends on feeling a measure of success and on being aware of making progress, even when we are far from getting things right.

Do you think students will question why they should work hard if they are not going to get marks? I have heard some people express this fear. This attitude reduces teaching to the level of animal training, where someone dishes out a dead fish for every trick a seal does. If students are working only for marks and teacher-approval, this seriously indicts our system. What will happen out of school? If learning offers no intrinsic rewards, then we will seek to learn nothing. If reading and writing have no purposes other than $B+$, then we have no motivation for literacy.

We cannot learn anything unless we ourselves can judge how we are doing. I judge my progress as a pianist by noting whether what I play sounds right to me, and if it sounds any better than it did the last time I played it. If I need someone to tell me every time I make a mistake, then I might as well give up. I certainly don't need my errors totaled up into a score – or my successes either, for that matter.

Whenever we assign a task that the student knows will be evaluated, we are setting up a test situation. But how much can we learn by taking a test? This is not the time to take risks, to try something new, to practise something we are not yet good at.

For evaluation to help the learner, it must be an integral part of the learning experience. We need to know how we are doing while we are doing it, not later. Then we have a chance to figure out how to do it better. When I am learning something new, I need someone who understands what I am trying to do and can help me do it better, then will get out of the way while I practise on my own. I don't need a critic; I need a coach.

In the real world of learning, self-evaluation is a constant part of what we do. When we first got on a two-wheeled bike, we did not sit down for some skills instruction first, nor did we need an adult's assessment of our performance. Certainly, a few words of praise and encouragement made us feel good, perhaps even convinced us to try again, but we did not need to be told that we were wobbling or falling off. We assessed our own progress as we went along, and adjusted our performance accordingly.

When I play golf, I have a score at the end of the round, which may be better or worse than previous scores. That score certainly has the power to make or break my day. But if I want to learn how to play golf better, that number isn't going to help. Listen to any golfer at the nineteenth hole, and you will get a complete rundown on exactly which shots worked well, which didn't, and how blind fate intervened. We know with every swing whether the swing went well or not, whether we should try something different next time, and whether we need help or instruction.

The best evaluator I ever had in my life was my piano teacher. Every week, Miss Every would give me my lesson, help me through my new pieces, then send me away to practise. For a whole week I practised on my own, without anyone looking over my shoulder, without anyone pointing out all my mistakes. I always knew when I had done something wrong. I also knew when I was getting better, which parts were more difficult and needed some extra practice, and what questions I needed to ask at the next lesson.

Practising when no one is listening is easiest; as soon as I had an audience, my anxiety increased and my skill decreased. (I used to notice this same phenomenon when teachers looked over my shoulder as they walked up and down the aisles – suddenly I could not formulate a sentence or think of an answer.)

When I went back for my next lesson I was expected to give my best performance of the pieces I had practised, and it was on this performance that I was evaluated. My skill was not judged on the average of all my attempts, but on the best performance I could give after as much practice as I chose to do. My achievement dictated how fast I progressed and what kinds of pieces my teacher gave me to play next. Once a year I took an external examination, and was graded according to a national standard.

We might well take this as a model for evaluation in the classroom. We can regard most of what the children do as practice, a time when reducing anxiety likely increases learning. During this time we can observe children's ways of working, look at the tasks they are engaged in, and assess what they are able to do, what help they need immediately. Perhaps monthly we can assess the best each child is able to accomplish. Three or four times a year, we can monitor each child's progress towards the outcomes we are aiming for.

As teachers, we might find it productive to help our students see ongoing evaluation as part of the process of doing a task. Students should know that the purpose of this type of evaluation is to help them succeed in the task. Having them understand this would likely support learning and prove to be more productive than having them see evaluation as an after-the-fact assessment of how well they did. Ongoing evaluation, made as we observe them at work, will also tell us far more about the students' learning processes.

I remember how ongoing evaluation worked particularly well in one of my Grade 5 classes. Students asked me to edit their writing. In the general course of responding to their writing, I was never one to write all over it – revisions were their job. But when I was asked to edit, I did what an editor does. I questioned parts that were unclear, located every spelling error, commented on their punctuation, indicated paragraphing, and generally covered their papers in red ink. And they were grateful! You see, when they asked me to edit, it was because they were planning to do a final draft, and they had learned that if errors still appeared in a final draft, it was not final – it needed to be done again.

The students saw editing as a positive, helping strategy, but would have seen correction as negative. I never had a student ask me to mark every error in a piece of writing, but they would insist on me doing this kind of editing. What I did would be the same in both cases; the difference was in the perception of the learner.

Assessment can help or hinder. We have control over what it does. We spend so much time on it these days, let's make sure it means something to someone.

> Evaluation must do more than support our teaching.
> It must be indistinguishable from it.

Making It Manageable

When I take my dog to the vet, I am always struck that the vet seems to have better records on the dog than I ever had on any of the students I taught. I used to feel guilty about this, until I remembered that the vet only sees the dog a couple of times a year, not every day. And he never has 30 dogs at once. However, he knows that keeping accurate records is important, not only as a statement of what the current situation is, but as a guide to planning future treatment.

One year I decided to try to keep detailed, anecdotal records on my students. I remembered that one early childhood education consultant of the past had advised me to jot down notes on scraps of paper during the day and put the notes into my apron pocket for transcription later on. The apron didn't seem to be quite my style. However, I set up a binder with a page for each student, and at the end of each day I jotted down observations. My record-keeping lasted three weeks. At that time, I looked back over what I had written and found it was totally irrelevant to my teaching. I decided I had better things to do with the time.

I have the greatest respect for those who can keep these kinds of records. I have never met such a teacher outside the covers of a book. Many of us founder on a reef of paperwork without really finding an effective way to record our students' achievements and needs.

Many of our newer methods of assessment and record-keeping are a reaction to the old system of marks and averages. We have gone through a period of viewing long, anecdotal records as modern and enlightened, and brief checklists as throwbacks to the past. We have done this with the best of intentions. Checklists were devised when we had a narrow range of low-level skills and right or wrong answers could be counted and scored. Now we want to assess students more precisely, so that we can more fairly represent what a child can do. We know that attitudes and ways of working are as important in the record as achievements. Also, we never know when someone will ask us about a child and we will have to justify our teaching and our assessments.

Any method of record-keeping that is too time-consuming and unwieldy will not last. It is therefore useless, no matter how enlightened. We need to be practical. In some cases, we must write a sentence or two of explanation to properly record an incident or event. Sometimes we will have to write a lengthy record. In many other cases, we can just slip a piece of student writing into a folder or put a check mark on a list of skills or achievements. Let's keep the lengthy reporting for times when it is really necessary.

Why not list skills we want students to develop as we plan themes, activities and projects? We might pick out some aspects of language for a special focus: locating information in reference books, formating a letter, making a chart, etc. Then, as we observe the students at work, listen as they talk, and look at their written work, we can use our checklist to note how each student is achieving the objectives. We can also use the checklist to prompt our own questioning and inspire extension activities.

At the end of the project or theme, we can do a more detailed assessment of work each student has produced. We can again check off what the student has done successfully on a checklist, make notes about what the student needs to learn, and store a sample or two of work in the student's portfolio.

Let us use a combination of all the many assessment and recording tools available to us. We can then focus our teaching better and monitor student progress in different ways.

We can document a student's progress in school by using the student's work portfolio, anecdotal comments, and checklists of achievements and accomplishments – let's not fill paper for the sake of looking efficient and modern.

Records of our students' achievements
are the milestones and signposts
pointing the path for future learning.

13

Parents: What Are Their Concerns?

Sending the Right Messages Home

When you ask your children what they did in school today, what do they typically answer? If they are like most children, they say, "Nothing." Why is this?

Well, it may just mean they have had enough of school for one day and don't want to think about it any more. We may not want to talk about our day, either, once we are at home and ready to relax. I wonder, though, if the children really think they have done nothing worth telling about. How many times can parents hear that without believing it too?

At the end of an activity, day, or unit of study, I can't remember ever asking my students what they felt they had learned. I wonder how often I asked myself what I thought the students had learned. Do we always take it on faith that if we conceived the activity well, then learning must have taken place?

Parents learn more about our classrooms from their children than they will ever learn from us. The messages the children take home reflect their own perceptions of what has happened and what they have learned. If parents do not understand what we are doing in our classrooms, then we have a problem. If the children do not understand why they are doing what they are doing, and do not know what they are learning, or what they are striving towards, then we have a disaster.

We do not have to leave perceptions to chance. We can provide time for students to reflect on and talk about what they are learning, thereby helping them recognize their own progress and enabling us to send them home with some concrete information to share with their parents.*

- We can make sure students know the purpose of an activity before they embark on it and review what they have learned or discovered from doing it. Classrooms tend to be places where students engage in many activities throughout the day. The purpose is not the activity, but some kind of end-product. Both we and the students should know what this purpose is and focus on it. I would like a student to be able to say, "I learned how to divide up my report into chapters today," or "I learned how to look up words I don't know how to spell."
- We can give children access to language with which to talk about their learning. Any student, even a six-year-old, can understand the writing process and possibly explain why some writing has uncorrected misspellings and messy handwriting. If the student cannot explain why, he or she probably does not understand the process. If children routinely talk about "first draft" and "editing" in the classroom, they will be able to use these terms at home as well.
- When students take work home, we can give them some hints and pointers about what is significant, and what might interest their parents.
  - "When your parents read this piece of writing, show them how you took all the bits of information and sorted them into sections to build your paragraphs."
  - "Why don't you ask your parents to look particularly at the verbs you used? Tell them how you looked for words to give stronger images."
- When students take work home, suggest ways they can enlist their parents' help with it.
  - "Perhaps your parents would help you put your information in the right order, ready for you to write your next draft."
  - "You might ask your parents to help you proofread for spelling errors. Perhaps they have a dictionary at home and could help you to find the correct spellings."

When a student experiences success, invite parents in to share the joy. Doing so is especially desirable when the student has success infrequently. You can send home a note: "Tonio has

---

* For more about reflecting on learning, see chapter 7.

created a display to show what he discovered about his rock collection. Can you come to school on Thursday afternoon? Tonio will be making a presentation to the class then." "Marla will be reading her poem during our assembly on Friday. Would you like to come along and help us celebrate?" Even if parents cannot attend, they will be learning what you value and noting their children's achievements. After this, what child can say he or she did nothing in school today?

You can also communicate directly with parents, letting them know how they can help at home. Doing this will show them that you care about skills and have a variety of ways for their children to learn and practise them.

- Send home a letter with a piece of a child's first-draft writing. Explain what the focus was, which aspects of writing the child is now learning, and which ones you will deal with at a later time.
- Send home instructions about word games to play in the car and at home. You could even spend time at a curriculum night showing parents how to play word games, spelling games, etc. Some of the students could help with this.
- When you come across a good book of games or puzzles, send the name home.
- When children are collecting words for a spelling pattern in school, let them ask their parents to add words to the list at home. In this way, parents will see how their children are learning to spell by recognizing patterns and structures.

The best way to make parents feel comfortable with your program is to invite them to visit your room. Even casual visitors will go back and talk to their friends about what you are doing.

Communicating Effectively

When I first began teaching, we sent home reports three times a year. The report form listed subjects, with a space for a term mark, an examination mark and a brief comment. In preparation for writing this report, we kept marks books and averaged the marks for the report.

Parents knew to the exact percentage point how well their children were doing, and whether they were better or worse than last time – or than the child next door.

We teachers knew this was an illusion. One year I moved from an inner-city school where I had taught Grade 7 to an upper-middle-class neighbourhood to teach Grade 4. The new neighbourhood was the kind where the deprived child had to make do with an above-ground pool. For several years, I had been comfortably writing "average," "above average" and "below average" on report cards. Now I found that my Grade 4 students could out-perform the Grade 7s in almost every respect. This started me wondering: what was average? When I asked around, someone told me to look at city and national norms. Should I have marked every student "below average"?

We knew, too, that marks were subjective: 73 percent from one teacher was not necessarily better than 65 percent from another teacher. I remember one professor in university announcing at the opening session that he never gave more than 80 percent.

We decided, as a profession, that percentages did not provide the best or fairest way to determine success or failure. We introduced letter grades instead. So those students who used to have 80 percent now had *A*, who had had 70 percent had *B*, and so on down the line. We were doing the same thing, but we were calling it by a different name.

A generation later, we decided that letter grades did not really let a parent know much about a child's progress or achievement. Our classrooms had changed, our skills were more complex, we had a better understanding of our students as individuals. Because we did not want to penalize children who were less able, we downplayed their problems and deficiencies and concentrated on their successes. We meant well, but many parents did not discover that their child was below average or had any kind of problem or difficulty until late in the child's school life. Then, failure began to loom. We wanted a new way to explain and describe what our students could do. We developed the anecdotal report.

We could now write about a child's interaction with peers, developmental stage, willingness to participate, and so on, using catch phrases that no parent could understand, and few cared about. We sat up night after night trying to express the same platitudes in different words on each report so the reports would seem individual. Some schools developed a list of set phrases for their computers, so teachers could punch in a key and select the phrases they wanted. I wondered why I went to so much trouble, though, when the first question a parent always asked at the interview was, "Well, how's he doing?"

We can view these Stages of Development of the Report Card from two different perspectives. From our point of view as teachers, we have moved from a system of arbitrary marks and grades to a report card that allows us to express what a child can do, and to record progress and development on many different levels, including social, physical and intellectual. From the parents' point of view, we have gone from a precise record of achievements and scores to a page full of teacher jargon they cannot understand. We have had a breakdown in communications.

None of us wants to return to a reliance on marks and scores. We want to move on, not backwards. We want a method of reporting that allows us to be fair and that does not result in children being compared with one another. But parents have a right to know how their children are doing. The children have a right to know, too. There is no reason we cannot report accurately and humanely at the same time. Surely we can say a child cannot yet read without it sounding like a moral deficiency or a social disease.

One of the problems with older reports was that skills got more attention than we thought they deserved. We would typically have one line for Creative Writing, one line for Comprehension, and seven or eight lines for Phonics, Word Attack, Spelling, Punctuation, Handwriting, and so on. This structure placed the emphasis in the wrong place.

More recently we tried to overcome this problem by grouping skills into such categories as Composition and Transcription. Sometimes, in our zeal to put writing skills in their proper perspective, we have neglected to comment on transcription skills at all; we have focused totally on creativity. While we may think this emphasis is fair, parents can easily draw the conclusion that we do not value skills. When we report to parents, we must make sure the skills receive their due focus.

I have found it helpful to look at writing skills in several categories:

composition	variety of modes, quality of ideas/topics
language use	vocabulary, audience awareness, sentence structure, grammatical sense
organization	clarity, sequence, paragraphing

spelling/punctuation	concepts and patterns used in the writing
presentation	formats, handwriting, neatness

By categorizing in this way, I could try to demonstrate the usual focus at different stages in the writing process, while reassuring parents that I was monitoring their child's growth in all areas.

When parents feel they are not getting accurate information, they demand a return to a system they felt more comfortable with. Such a return would do none of us any good. We have made the mistake of taking away many of the supports of the past, traditions with which people felt comfortable, without making it obvious what we have put in their place. We forgot the first rule of airplane wing-walking – never let go of one strut until you have a firm grasp on the next.

Let's make our report cards a place for plain talk which we all understand. If we feel we cannot do this satisfactorily in written form, and I doubt we can, let's encourage meetings with parents so we can answer all questions. In one of my schools, reports were not sent home at all – parents had to come and pick them up. This gave us the chance to show the child's work, answer parents' questions, and explain the abbreviated version we wrote in the report. In some schools, reports are written afterwards, as a summary of the discussion with the parents at the interview. It might be interesting to see such a summary written by the parents – how do they perceive their child's progress and achievement? We could also ask the child for a summary.

If we do not keep parents fully in the picture, then we will continue to have a credibility gap, with a loss of public confidence resulting. Parents need to know where their children are succeeding, where they are experiencing difficulty, what we are doing about it, and how they can help.

Aren't these the same things we need to know to teach effectively? If we cannot answer these questions for ourselves, we cannot teach effectively.

> People vital to a child's learning:
> **the child**
> **the parents**
> **the teacher**
> – in that order

14

Conclusion: Where Do We Go From Here?

A Common-Sense Approach

> Down, down, down. Would the fall *never* come to an end? "I wonder how many miles I've fallen by this time!" she said aloud. "I must be getting somewhere near the centre of the earth. Let me see: that would be four thousand miles down, I think – " (for, you see, Alice had learned several things of this sort in her lessons in the schoolroom, and though this was not a *very* good opportunity for showing off her knowledge, as there was no one to listen to her, still it was good practice to say it over)"– Yes, that's about the right distance – but then I wonder what Latitude or Longitude I've got to?" (Alice had no idea what Latitude was, or Longitude either, but thought they were nice grand words to say.)

This excerpt from *Alice's Adventures in Wonderland* brings to mind the way schools used to be – much of the day spent in rote-memorization which the children soon forgot. The public perception that skills teaching was more important and more effective in those days is a myth; only those with very selective memories about what went on in classrooms believe it. Returning to the teaching methods of the past will not equip children to cope with the changing world they live in.

I began this book by saying I was going to reflect on my own experience in the classroom and try to make sense of it all. One impression overrides all others: we should be proud of our achievements in education. Our schools are more humane, more relevant, and more universal than they have ever been. We teachers do our job better because, instead of just repeating the experiences of the past, we have learned our craft, both from researchers and from our students. Like our students, we have learned to question, to reason and to problem-solve.

During my time in schools, education has probably gone through more changes than in all its past history combined. We teachers have been bombarded with new information, new methodologies, new pressures. Often we have jumped or been pushed into new ways of working without a thorough understanding of what we are doing and why. These superficial understandings have often led us to abandon old ways without replacing them with new and better ones. Remember the first rule of wing-walking.* Hence the so-called pendulum swing.

Rather than picking sides or running from one side of the ship to the other, we need to take a more balanced view and make full use of what we have learned about learning, about children, and about teaching.

We now do more than merely impart knowledge. Modern technology has advanced too far for that to be either possible or necessary. We must understand the skills of the subjects we teach, in all their complexity, and make informed choices about the most appropriate way to help our students learn and apply them. If we begin with the children, and employ all the skills we have learned, then we will succeed. Child-centred teaching and skills teaching can go hand in hand.

We must give our students the tools with which to fathom their evolving world. These tools are the skills with which to learn, think and communicate.

> We are, above all, teachers of skills.

* See page 100.

Index